PRAISE FOR *BEAR BOY*

"In this compelling, honest, and moving story, Justin Barker proves that one kid can make a *big* difference. Old and young, rich and poor, black and white, LGBTQ and straight—we *all* have the power to change the lives of animals for the better. Thank you, Justin, for showing us what creativity, commitment, and compassion can accomplish for our sweet green earth and *all* its creatures!"
—**Sy Montgomery, NYT bestselling author, *The Soul of an Octopus***

"An empowering story of a young man who discovered his words count, his actions count, and he counts. This is his story of finding a way to liberate incarcerated bears—Ursula and Brutus—and finding his own identity. A book changed him and this book may change you. Delightful in umpteen ways." —**Ingrid Newkirk, founder and president, People for the Ethical Treatment of Animals**

"A truly empowering story of compassion, activism, and self-discovery. Justin takes us through his inspirational journey of overcoming obstacles with persistence and passion to make a tangible difference for animals."—**Jasmin Singer, author, *Fabulous Vegan* and *Always Too Much and Never Enough***

"*Bear Boy* is a fantastic read—deeply engaging with twists and turns, high stakes, and big heart. I'm so grateful to Justin Barker for telling this story—and for having lived it."—**Michelle Tea, bestselling author, *Valencia* and *Against Memoir***

"*Bear Boy* is a blueprint and inspiration for young animal lovers everywhere that one small, insistent voice can have a big impact. This book would have been a godsend when I was a queer, animal-loving kid."—**Nicole Georges, graphic memoirist, *Fetch* and *Calling Dr. Laura***

"Justin sets an example for what a motivated young person can do to impact their community and the world. This story shows that no person is too young to become an activist and makes me proud of my work in environmental activism. Written with honesty and humor, it's fun to tag along as Justin fights his long battle to save Brutus and Ursula. We need more stories like this."
—**Jamie Margolin, cofounder, Zero Hour; author, *Youth to Power***

BEAR BOY

THE TRUE STORY OF A BOY, TWO BEARS, AND THE FIGHT TO BE FREE

Justin Barker

Foreword by **Jane Goodall**

BRUTUS & URSULA
San Francisco, California

For permission requests, contact the publisher at
info@brutusursula.com

ISBN: 978-1-7360843-2-8

Edited by Jennie Nash
Cover art by Doaly
Interior design by Carla Weise

Library of Congress Control Number: 2020951122

Names: Barker, Justin, author. | Goodall, Jane, 1934- writer of
supplementary textual content.
Title: Bear boy: the true story of a boy, two bears, and the fight to be
free / by Justin Barker; with foreword by Jane Goodall.
Description: First edition. | San Francisco, California : Brutus &
Ursula, LLC, 2021. | Interest age level: 012-018. | Summary: Bear
boy is a coming-of-age story of how two bears inspire one boy to
stand up, question authority, fight for animals and discover the
power of activism;--Provided by publisher.
Identifiers: ISBN 9781736084304 (hardcover)
| ISBN 9781736084328 (paperback)
| ISBN 9781736084311 (ebook)
Subjects: LCSH: Barker, Justin. | Animal rights activists--Biography--
Juvenile literature. | Gay teenagers--Biography
Juvenile literature. |Coming of age--Juvenile literature. |
Self-esteem in adolescence--Juvenile literature. | Young adult
literature. | CYAC: Barker, Justin.| Animal rights activists--
Biography. | Gay teenagers--Biography. |Coming of age.
| Self-esteem. | LCGFT: Autobiographies.
Classification: LCC HV4716.B37 A3 2021 (print)
| LCC HV4716.B37 (ebook) |DDC 179.3092--dc23

Brutus & Ursula, LLC
530 Divisadero St #778
San Francisco, CA 94117

www.brutusursula.com

To the '90s

This is a work of nonfiction. No characters have been invented, but some names have been changed. In some cases, I have compressed events. All conversations come from my recollections. I have retold them in a way that evokes the feeling and meaning of what was said, so the essence of the dialogue is accurate. I have described some daydreams that did not occur in real life but are honest reflections of what was going on in my head—which was a lot. I have done my best to tell a truthful story.

—*Justin*

FOREWORD

The world we live in can be a very depressing place. Especially for those of us who are concerned about the environment and about the way animals are often treated so badly, without respect for their personalities, their emotions, their "beingness." At the same time, there are so many amazing people out there, doing amazing projects, changing the world for the better. And many of those activities are tackled by young people, sometimes quite young children.

I heard about Justin Barker when he was just fourteen years old. Known as "Bear Boy," he was profiled in an article that described his determination to free two bears from their tiny prison cage in a zoo, and all the setbacks that he was struggling to overcome. And when, some years later, I heard that he had finally, against all odds, succeeded, I sent him a postcard to congratulate him.

By that time, I was already spending most of each year travelling around the world, trying to raise awareness, to encourage people to take action to save our planet before it is too late. It was before the days of email and texting and tweeting, and I often used to send little handwritten notes to thank people, to congratulate them for a job well done. Perhaps I sent about five hundred of these little notes a year. Because people fighting hard fights in sometimes uncaring environments need all the encouragement they can get. Because so many give up their dreams.

As a child I always loved and respected animals, and when I was ten years old, after reading *Tarzan of the Apes* and *The Story of Doctor Doolittle*, I dreamed of going to Africa, living with wild animals, and writing books about them. Everyone laughed at me—how could I possibly do that? We had very little money and girls did not do that sort of thing. Only my mother and family did not laugh. My mother simply said that I would have to work very hard, take advantage of all opportunities, and never give up. It is a message I share with young people all around the world.

A few weeks ago, I was checking my zillions of emails and, to my surprise and delight, there was one from Bear Boy. He had just finished writing a book, sharing his story with the world. Immediately, I asked him to send me a copy. I planned to simply glance through it—I had so much work to do. But I simply couldn't put it down. It is fascinating and compelling reading, a story told in excellent prose with a perfect balance between Justin's passion for justice, his determination to free the bears, and the problems he went through and overcame along the way, including in his personal life.

This is a book that will encourage young people to follow their dreams, to work hard to achieve a goal no matter how often they are told it is impossible. It is a book that illustrates one of the things I tell everyone—that each of us has a role to play in making this a better world. It is a book that may ignite a passion in readers to tackle an issue that has bothered them, but about which they felt powerless to do anything. It is a book that gives one hope for the future of our planet. Because Justin's story provides a perfect example of how one person, with enough determination, with the ability to carry on in spite of problems that seem insurmountable at the time, in spite of teasing and bullying, can in the end succeed.

I hope that you, the reader, will be inspired to take action, to do something to make this a better world. Follow your dream. Follow your heart. Because if Bear Boy defeated the odds, so can you.

—Jane Goodall,
Founder, Jane Goodall Institute, UN Messenger of Peace

The hallways at Harriet Eddy Middle School were the worst place to be. It was a hormone highway full of intimidation, insults, and threats. When I passed by certain kids, I knew what was coming. Jason would always scream, "Sabretooth" at me and make some weird video game noises. My canines were growing in above the rest of my tooth line and I did sort of look like a Sabretooth. I was fat and my chest filled my shirt better than Cheryl's, who clearly hadn't started puberty. She was the school newspaper editor and always threatening to publish her views. She had a certain way she held her hands over her head when she described what the headline was going to be: "Bra found in Booby Boy's Locker," she would say, pointing at my chest and laughing hysterically.

Daniel always taunted me with a question I dreaded most: "Are you a fag?"

I had been hearing that question since I was four years old when the kids across the street discovered I was in ballet class, and then again in second grade when I cried on a school field trip to the zoo, and then every day in seventh grade when I passed by Daniel and the jerks he hung out with. I wasn't exactly sure what "fag" meant or why that taunt followed me in particular, but I had a feeling it wasn't good. I just tried to ignore it. I tried ignoring all of the terrible words that zoomed around those halls, but in seventh grade when a large glob of slimy spit landed on my face, I lost it. I threw my backpack down and charged towards the kid who'd done it. "Do you want to fight?" I repeated over and over.

I thought my height and anger would scare him. I thought he might answer yes. I was betting on no, but I was not expecting a punch to my face. My glasses flew across the hallway. The guy's blurred fist came into focus again and again. Kids hurried in our direction. "Fight! Fight! Fight!" they chanted. I eventually got the guy into a headlock and some teacher broke up the scene. If I had known he was on the junior boxing team, I would have probably just let him spit on me.

He was suspended, and I spent the afternoon at Dr. Rolofson's. "Thank goodness you have braces," the orthodontist told me, as he squeezed my top lip and removed a blood-soaked cotton swab. "You would have completely lost your front ones if we hadn't installed these puppies."

My mom was pretty angry at me when she picked me up at school to take me to the doctor's—a remnant of the argument we'd had that morning at breakfast. We were often angry at each other over everything and nothing. She softened a bit that day after hearing the whole story and witnessing my front teeth getting thrust back into my skull at the orthodontist's; we shared an Oreo cookie soft serve at our favorite yogurt shop on the way back. As we drove home, I noticed the road was shimmering, as it often did in late May. Mirages in the Sacramento Valley meant two things—that school was almost out for summer and that the 100-degree days were on their way. Even through those heat waves, Elk Grove was nowhere near as magical as the images conjured by mirages on TV—nothing could hide the endless pavement, minivans, or sea of beige tract housing.

I was so happy school was almost over because I had big plans for that summer of '95: to avoid the neighborhood kids, eat tons of Honey Bunches of Oats, sleep as much as I could, and catch every episode of *Clarissa Explains It All.*

I loved all the shows on Nickelodeon, but *Clarissa* was my favorite. Clarissa was only a year older than me at fourteen and we had a ton in common—a brother who was obsessed with money, ex-hippie parents, a mom whose cooking was well-intentioned but rarely good. We both loved journalism and had pretty cool rooms. She had much better style than me and had a best friend; I waited for the ladder to hit the windowsill of Clarissa's second-story bedroom every episode because that meant her friend was there. Sam would climb through with his skateboard and Clarissa, sometimes without even looking over, would always greet him the same way: "Hi, Sam," she would say to a distinct guitar chord. I was really envious of Sam—a friend Clarissa could rely on, someone to confide in, someone who would look on the bright side when she was having a tough day, someone to talk to after a big fight with her mom.

There was none of that in my life. I tried making friends so many times, but it always ended in misery— Yvonne moved to Sunnyvale, Aaron's parents forced us to stop hanging out because I wasn't a Jehovah's Witness, Matt told me he wanted friends who liked sports,

Derek started hanging out with the cool kids at another school. I seemed doomed to be the kid everyone avoided or taunted.

Home wasn't much better.

My mom controlled almost everything I did. She had a never-ending list of chores for me. Sometimes I wondered if she birthed me just to do housework. I couldn't do anything unless chores were done, and the list was so long I could hardly do anything. My room had to be spotless, I had to clean the bathroom, vacuum downstairs, wash the dishes, do my own laundry, mow the lawn, and pull the weeds. On top of all that, I got restricted at least once a month for talking back. She'd warn me to stop talking back, but I never listened. Her upper lip would tighten when she didn't like something I said—and I said a lot of things she didn't like. She called me disrespectful and I called her many rude things and slammed many doors, especially when she'd give me obscenely long restrictions. They would often start as days but would quickly extend to weeks and months. Because I didn't have any friends and didn't leave the house much, restriction meant I had to hand over my radio, unscrew the cable cords for the TV, and stand by helplessly as my dad changed the AOL passwords.

My dad was a total pushover, and he would go along with whatever my mom said, even when she gave me cruelly long restrictions. He was a counselor at a school for emotionally disturbed kids, so by the time he got home he didn't really have much patience for emotion or disturbances.

My brother, Shane, was six years older than me and had recently moved out, leaving me as the only child at home. We lived in a new, two-story house in Elk Grove. It had a five-foot-tall elm tree in the front yard and a four-foot magnolia in the back. Our house had a living room *and* a family room. The whole place was covered in floral wallpaper, silk plants, and family antiques. We had two cars, a big TV, and a Mac computer, and weekly trips to Costco filled our pantry. Most people would have said it was a nice house.

I should've appreciated it, but I hated living there.

Our neighborhood was crammed between the farmlands of Elk Grove and the sprawling housing tracts of South Sacramento. The air reeked of manure and the nighttime scared me to death. When I was nine years old, someone broke into our car, opened our garage door, and came into our house while we were sleeping—stealing my mom's purse, our Nintendo system, and our van.

Sometimes, I'd wake up in the middle of the night to police helicopter spotlights in our backyard and other times to toe-curling catfights.

Six months after that first break-in, when I woke up to tires screeching down the street and my parents running down the stairs screaming that our car had been stolen again, my sense of safety disappeared as well. That night I retreated to my closet. I moved my shoes and created a small nest of comforters and pillows. I slept that way for much of my adolescence. I figured that if anyone was going to come into our house, they would never guess I was in the closet.

My obsession with the local TV news and its daily reports of kidnappings, murders, and break-ins probably didn't help matters. About the same year our cars were stolen, I met Noel Cisneros, a TV reporter from KOVR 13, who happened to follow my family as we delivered Thanksgiving meals to the homebound elderly. Noel and her cameraman drove in our van with us and Noel sat in the very back seat with me. I fell in love with her and her job—the lights, the microphones, her own personal cameraman, the precision of her words, her singsongy intonations.

After we saw ourselves on the news that Thanksgiving night, watching the news became a ritual for me. Every night at five p.m. I flipped on Channel 13 just in time to catch the opening theme song. I knew every reporter by name and I eagerly waited to see what story Noel was covering each night. At five thirty I would run into the bathroom and practice in the mirror, holding a hairbrush to my mouth: "In Sacramento, Justin Barker, KOVR 13 News." I would repeat it over and over, using the deepest voice I could muster. I had no idea how useful that nightly practice would become over the next few years—imagining myself on camera, speaking to big audiences.

I felt as comfortable as I could feel in my parent's house watching Clarissa and Noel on TV and spending nights sleeping in the closet. But during that first week of summer vacation after seventh grade, my dad laid down a threat that forced me out of my comfort zone and would end up changing the course of my life.

"I'm going to be working summer school this year," he proclaimed, making a sharp turn into the parking lot of Almost Perfect, a used bookstore where my parents were regulars.

"What are *your* plans, buddy?"

Before I even had a chance to respond, he added, "You can't just sit around the house watching TV!"

If I couldn't sit around the house watching TV, I would have to face the scorching heat, the neighborhood water gun fights, and the bullies who teased me. As I walked towards the bookstore, all of the excitement about my summer drained out of my body.

I never liked going to the used bookstore. My parents would spend way too long there. Trading in books. Asking the clerks about their favorites. Perusing the different racks. Sitting in the ratty chairs reading the first few pages of a million books. I really wished my parents weren't so cheap and would just shop at a normal bookstore—they smelled better and had books I would actually want to read. Instead, we shopped the tattered books and the terrible tastes of the suburbanites who surrounded us.

My dad and I entered the familiar doors of Almost Perfect. A brass bell above the door rang as we entered. *Trade credits must be used at least one time per year,* said a handwritten sign taped to the register. My dad set a stack of books on the counter to trade and headed to his favorite section: westerns. He could get through three in a week.

I headed towards the youth section and plopped down on the stained beanbag chair and half-heartedly stared at the shelves. Among the browned, worn books that filled my vision, something caught my eye: a bright pink book that actually looked brand new. I grabbed it. *Kids Can Save the Animals: 101 Easy Things to Do.*

As I flipped through the short chapters, I couldn't believe what I was reading. I always liked learning about animals in *National Geographic.* I loved the story of Jane Goodall and her chimpanzees. I was aware that rain forests were being cut down at a rapid rate. I always made sure to switch off the lights and turn off the water when I brushed my teeth. I knew that we all needed to do our small part to help the environment, but I had no idea that one of my favorite meals—turkey with mashed potatoes smothered in gravy—was made of an actual animal.

I was really confused. No one ever told me that the food we ate—meatballs, chicken salads, pork chops, ribs, hamburgers, baloney—didn't just come from the grocery store. They never explained that the strips, grounds, and slices were just the end of a long factory line, that the colorful packaging was just a facade, that animals were raised in small cages, endured horrific abuse, and were slaughtered to make the meals we ate. I couldn't believe what I was reading and that no one had told me the truth—not my mom, who was a nurse, nor my dad, who I thought of as so informed. I was embarrassed that it took me so long to figure it out. I continued reading, struggling to catch every word as tears welled in my eyes. I had to shake my head in disbelief.

Luckily, there was an escape from the horror story in which I was an unwitting participant. Just as the title of the book proposed, I could help animals by making different choices. At the end of the chapter, there was an invitation that I accepted: to go vegetarian.

I repeated the words in my head a few times. I was preparing for what I would have to say at dinner that night. I said it again out loud. "I'm vegetarian." I had never said or felt anything with such certainty, and after that moment, I never ate meat again.

My dad was surprised when I added the book to the stack of yellowed paperbacks he was trading for. "You found something?"

I nodded and he paid for the book. But I was so angry, I could hardly look at him.

On the way home, I finally exploded. "Why did you force me to eat pork chops when you knew they were pigs?" I asked, without pausing to hear his response. "You know that they live in cages too small to turn around? You know they are dragged onto trucks and sent to be killed? You know that they are smarter than dogs?" He focused on the road "Dad. Why?" I wondered if his silence was regret or if he was zoning out like he often did.

"You should talk to your mom," he finally responded When we got home, my mom was in the kitchen. I didn't have to ask what was for dinner because we had been eating the same damn thing for what felt like an eternity—chicken salad. I walked into the kitchen. "I'm not eating your chicken salad anymore," I said before she could turn around from the stove to greet me.

"Well, that's what we are having for dinner," she said, irritated.

"I will go hungry, then," I retorted. I was ready for a fight. "You have been feeding me this nasty chicken salad every day for the last year and I'm done. I'm vegetarian, and I'm never eating meat ever again. Ever."

She softened when she heard those words. My mom was always into the latest fad diets—trying to keep us healthy and lose weight. Chicken salad was the latest, and lentil burgers were before that. Our cupboards were filled with amaranth crackers, rice cakes, and fresh ground peanut butter that would get caught in your throat. She walked over to the table where I had sat down with my book. "Honey," she said, "I've always wanted to be a vegetarian. I just thought you kids needed protein."

Feeling a surge of hope, I grabbed the book, flipped to a chapter, and referred to a bullet point I had seen earlier. I read it verbatim: "'We can get all the protein we need from vegetables, tofu, nuts, rice, wheat, potatoes, and beans.'"

My mom found a box of falafel mix in the cupboard and made it for dinner that night. My dad was left to eat the large portion of chicken strips my mom had cooked for all of us.

"We'll have to go shopping at the natural food co-op tomorrow evening," Mom said. "Everything is vegetarian there."

That initial step towards helping animals was a profound one for me. It was the first time in my life that things felt right: I was making a decision that had nothing to do with my parents and I could tell that they supported it in some way. I closed my closet door that night and dozed off thinking about all the vegetarian food we were going to buy at the store the next day, and the next morning, instead of reading the back of the Honey Bunches of Oats box during breakfast, I read another chapter in my book.

There I found some actions even a thirteen-year-old kid who didn't want to leave the house could take. "Can't get to the next animal rights protest?" it read. "Fur companies, cruel cosmetic companies, and others often have '800' numbers that you can call for free. When you have politely stated your opinion to the operator, ask to be transferred to a supervisor. The longer you talk, the better for the animals."

I grabbed the phone off the wall and dialed the first number on the list.

"Thank you for calling Neiman Marcus. How can I help you?" the voice said.

I was nervous, so I followed the script in the book. "Hi. I just got your catalog in the mail and I couldn't believe you're *still* selling fur. Animals are killed for their fur in awful ways and they deserve their lives, just like we do."

I called Gillette and said, "There's no excuse for blinding and poisoning animals."

I called Georgia-Pacific and said, "Your paper products are not welcome in my house until you stop buying trees chopped down in the rain forest."

I was just following the scripts in the book. We never received the Neiman Marcus catalog, we only bought Kirkland Signature toilet paper, and I was pretty sure there were only BIC razors in my parents' bathroom—but when I spotted a very familiar store on the list of companies that sold fur, it felt personal. My mom was obsessed with shopping at Nordstrom and she dragged me there any chance she got. There was no 800 number for Nordstrom, but I'd seen my mom dial the store enough that I knew exactly where to find the number. I grabbed the floral embroidered phone book out of the drawer next to the phone and dialed the scribbled number.

"Nordstrom Arden Fair. How can I direct your call?" the operator asked.

"I shop at Nordstrom at least once a week," I said, "and I can't believe you sell fur! Animals are killed for their fur in awful ways and I need to talk with someone there who can explain how Nordstrom justifies killing animals for profit."

The woman politely asked if I could hold and when she came back on the line, she informed me she was transferring me to someone who could answer my question.

After a brief moment of jazz, a man answered the phone. "This is Jim Nordstrom."

Oh my gosh, I thought, *Nordstrom is a real person, and I was just transferred to him.*

"Hello?" he asked, to my silence.

"My mom takes me to Nordstrom all of the time," I said. "I just read in a book that you sell fur and I wanted to call to see why you think that's okay."

He asked me my name, age, and then did something no one had done. He thanked me for calling. "I agree with you, Justin," he said. "Animals shouldn't be killed for their furs. My family would never buy fur, but we have plenty of people who want them. We have to cater to all types of customers and keep our shareholders happy."

"Harrods of London stopped selling fur a few years ago," I read from the book. "You could do the same thing if you really cared, *Jim*," I emphasized his name just like he did mine. I appreciated that he took the time to listen to me, but I found it pretty pathetic that he would choose money over his ethics. "I hope you can wash that blood off your hands one day," I said with the defiant tone my mom loathed. "I'm going to convince my mom and her friends not to shop at Nordstrom until you do." I hung up the phone on Jim like the rest of the operators had done to me. I knew there was no way I could convince my mom to stop shopping at Nordstrom. "It's the only place that carries size eleven shoes," she would say. I also knew that she would put me on restriction if I talked to her the way

I talked to Jim. And for hanging up on her? It would have been two months long!

I felt fired up after that call. Someone had actually listened to me and I used the "sharp tongue" that got me in so much trouble at home to speak up for animals who desperately needed a voice. I was jumping up and down in the kitchen, spinning in excitement. I settled down to see what would unfold in the coming chapters and flipped to one called "Born Free, Bored Stiff."

The chapter began: "Zoos started long ago as menageries—collections of exotic wild animals kept by kings and emperors. Showmen decided that the public would pay to see fierce tigers and weird monkeys, so city zoos were built." My heart sank at the idea of animals being snatched from their families in Africa and brought to terrible places like the Valley. As I read on about the problems with zoos, a horrible memory came flooding back from second grade.

Our teacher told us that our class was adopting Penny, a black-footed cat, from the zoo. I became obsessed with Penny and would stare at her photo that was pinned next to the thermometer that indicated how much my class had raised for her adoption fee. The teacher promised that once we had raised enough money, we could go to the zoo to visit her. Twenty of us put twenty-five cents from our lunch money in a jar every day for three weeks until we raised seventy-five dollars. My favorite time of the day was science when we learned all about African animals, and we spent the entire week leading up to our field trip learning about black-footed cats.

It was a warm spring day when our trip to the zoo finally arrived. We stepped off the yellow bus in a single file. I was mortified to be wearing the exact same neon green shirt as the rest of the kids in my class. They read *Zoo Crew*. I tuned out our tour guide as we wandered through the zoo, passing by the many animals. "Blah, blah, blah hyenas. Zebras yadda, yadda." I just wanted to meet Penny.

Then, beyond the filthy hippo tank, pass the puke-green duck pond, the moment I had been waiting for arrived. The paint peeled off a sign that hung over the walkway: *Small Felines of Africa*. We moved past a long line of cages until the tour guide stopped our group. "This is

Penny," she said. "She is the black-footed cat you all raised money for."

We had learned that her species was nocturnal and slept most of the day. I had imagined she would be in a big sandy pit with well-shaded shadows for her midday naps. I pushed to the front of the group and spotted her in a concrete and metal cage that was only a little bigger than my closet. It was filled with dead tree branches, but I knew from our studies that she couldn't even climb. Her eyes were wide. She looked like a scared house cat trying to escape the sun *and* our glares. If she weren't locked in that hell, she would live on the sandy terrain of the Namibian savannahs. My palms began to sweat from my tight grip on the four-foot-tall fence that stood between us and her enclosure.

One of the kids shook the fence to taunt her. She jumped and cowered near the closed door at the back of her cage. Everyone, including the adults, laughed at her reaction—everyone, that is, except me. I felt so sad for Penny, such disappointment, such shock that anyone thought these conditions were okay. And the fact that she had just become the butt of a bully's cruel joke? Tears began to roll down my face.

"Look at Jus-*teen*!" squealed the same kid who had just taunted Penny, adding and then emphasizing an "e" at the end of my name. He turned everyone's attention to me. "What are you crying about?" he asked loudly, without an ounce of curiosity in his voice.

———

Six years later, at the start of summer, reading the truth about zoos made me realize that I *was* right to feel sad for Penny that day. Those kids and adults didn't get it and there *was* something wrong with staring and laughing at animals locked in cages thousands of miles from their natural homes. I also realized that I wasn't so different than Penny—that I, too, was trapped in a place I didn't want to be, enclosed by gender stereotypes and surrounded by bullies, with no end in sight.

The front door opened; my dad was home early from work. I sat there with my book. He looked surprised that I hadn't moved since breakfast *and* that I wasn't in front of the TV. "Dad," I blurted out, finally ready to answer the question he had asked me in the car on the way to the bookstore just the day before.

"I know what I'm gonna to do this summer."

2

"I'm gonna investigate what's happening at the Sacramento Zoo," I declared, chasing my dad up the stairs, desperate to tell him what I had just learned about the zoo industry. "Killer whales can live to be one hundred in the wild, but some only live for eighteen months when they are put in tanks. When animals—"

My dad slid the bathroom door closed, cutting me off.

I usually left him alone when he got home, but not on that day. I sat down on the floor and leaned against the his-and-hers sinks outside of the bathroom, raising my voice so he could hear me. I continued: "When animals get too old, they get sold to game farms where people pay to shoot them."

"Just give me ten minutes, Justin," Dad pleaded through the door. "I want to hear all about it, but I need a minute."

My dad had never sounded so pathetic and I figured this was a perfect moment to get him to agree to my request. "Fine. I just want to know if you'll take me to the zoo on your way to work tomorrow." I waited for a second and then barked his name. "Dad?"

"I can take you," he said. "We'll talk about it when I'm out."

I retreated downstairs and sat back down in the same chair where I had spent the entire morning. I reread the last paragraph. "You can be a zoo checker!" it said. I jumped back up and ran into my room to grab the reporter's notepad that Noel had given me. I started jotting down the list of things to look out for so that I could take notes the next day:

- Do the animals have enough water?
- Can they stand up, lie down, and move around comfortably?
- Do they look healthy?
- Are their coats shiny?
- Are the great apes active?

- Do the animals have company or things
  to do?
- Do the elephants and other large animals have
  rubbing posts or mounds?

My dad came walking down the stairs towards the kitchen. "So, what do you want to do at the zoo?" he asked.

"Have you heard of zoochosis?" I asked. Before he had the chance to answer, I read that section from the book out loud. "'Boredom, loneliness, and cramped conditions in zoos can cause psychological damage in animals—a condition called zoochosis. Watch out for behavior like pacing, circling, bar biting, neck twisting, self-mutilating, and overgrooming.'"

"Wow, that's depressing," my dad said. I was amazed that he really seemed to feel what I had been feeling. It made me realize that, while my dad loved eating meat, he also had a soft spot for animals.

"That is what I'm going to do," I said, holding up my notepad and showing him my notes. "Go undercover."

"And do what?" he asked with a slight chuckle.

I wasn't sure if my dad's laugh was from surprise or skepticism, but it didn't matter to me either way. "I'm going to investigate what's happening at the zoo, make sure the animals are being treated well, and see if any of them look like they have zoochosis."

My dad nodded and agreed to take me to the zoo the next morning. "You have to be ready by eight o'clock," he said, probably assuming that I would sleep in until ten a.m. as usual and would miss the ride.

The next morning, I was ready long before eight. I made myself a sandwich for lunch, and Dad gave me ten bucks for a ticket. When we got to the zoo, he double-parked, pulling up between two school buses, giving me just enough room to open the door and squeeze out.

"You need to be right here at three o'clock," he said.

I assured him I would be there on time and set off to do my work. I tucked in my striped polo, adjusted my glasses, and tightened the straps of my backpack over my shoulders. I didn't know what I would find on the other side of the turnstiles, but I felt a rush of excitement and a sense of freedom that I was out of the house and on a mission without my mom or dad around. I also knew I was safe from bullying at the zoo—if any of the kids I knew were there, they would probably be with their parents and little siblings. They couldn't soak me with water balloons or call me names, which were things that happened regularly on the streets outside my house. I walked through a large group of elementary school kids all in matching shirts. I realized I hadn't been to the zoo since second grade.

I bought my ticket, stuffed the three dollars and fifty cents change into my front pocket, clutched the map the cashier gave me, and pushed through the heavy turnstiles. I walked past a thatched roof gift shop towards a loud group of flamingos wading in the shallows of a big pond. A plastic banner—*Lake Victoria: Africa's Great Lake*—hung from the short, chain-link fence. I read the list of the birds that called this particular pond home and where they could be found in the wild: greater flamingos, native to Chile; hooded mergansers, and cinnamon teals, both native to America.

I pulled out my notebook and a pen. "African lake with no African birds," I noted.

I sat on a bench just opposite the flamingos. Some flapped their wings in an attempt to fly. The same group of school kids I passed outside approached the fence that stood between us and the bright pink birds. "They look so weird," a little girl yelled. "Look, that one is standing on one leg," a young boy said, and pointed and laughed. Nothing had changed since I was in second grade.

I had seven hours to spend at the zoo, so I studied my map in order to best plot out my day. I started counting how many exhibits there were and how much time I could spend at each one, keeping track of the numbers in my head: Lion, tiger, polar bear, chimpanzee, orangutan, kangaroo, fishing cat, serval, black-footed cat...

"Penny!" I cried. I slipped my notepad into my back pocket and followed the path towards the rear of the zoo where the map showed the small felines lived. There she was, in the same inadequate cage I had walked away from in tears six years prior. She scampered around the same path at the back of her cage, making repetitive circles over and over. Her fur was dull and matted. I stood there in disbelief. Nothing had changed in six years, but now I understood exactly what I was seeing: zoochosis. Years of living in cramped quarters, unable to hide from the day's sun, exposed to endless taunts and stares, had driven her to insanity. I had no tears for Penny this time, just anger. I made a silent promise to her that I would do something.

As I walked through the zoo, I was dismayed with what I discovered. A hippo wading in a filthy pool that could hardly contain its girth. A polar bear panting in a concrete grotto unable to escape the scorching summer sun. A hyena whose haunches were worn raw from pacing in circles around its small cage. A chimpanzee flinging its poop at the glass that kids pounded with their fists. Two cheetahs whose enclosure was too small for them to get a running start. It was a really horrible place—and it reminded me so much of the way I felt at home and in my lonely bubble at school.

As I observed each enclosure and documented what I saw, I discovered that most of the animals at the Sacramento Zoo showed signs of distress and were being held in enclosures far too small to meet their needs. I sat down to eat the veggie baloney sandwich I had made that morning and thought about what I would do with the remaining two hours I had until pickup.

I noticed that a woman in a khaki shirt and shorts had entered the cage across from where I sat and had started blasting the concrete ground with a water hose. I walked towards the front of the cage and tried getting her attention over the sound of the high-pressure spraying.

"Excuse me," I said politely. She didn't hear me, so I yelled, "Helllllo."

She twisted the nozzle of the hose shut and walked to the front of the cage. "Hi. Can I help you?" she asked.

"Yes," I said. "I'm concerned about the conditions here and I would like to know who I need to talk with about them."

"I was wondering what you were doing for so long at the hippo tank this morning," she said, smiling and nodding her head. "Good for you!" She pointed toward the back of the zoo. "If you follow that path all the way, you'll find the offices. Ask for Nancy Knight, she's the director of the zoo."

I was surprised by her friendliness and her encouraging words.

I followed the path to a building that had "Administration" painted on the door. I swung it open and was greeted with a blast of cold air. It was such relief after spending the entire day in the heat. A woman stood up and greeted me from behind a counter stacked tall with papers, the skull of an alligator, and a massive cast-off snake skin. I asked her if I could speak to Nancy Knight. She told me that Nancy was gone for the day and insisted that even if she was there that she was only available by appointment. I told her I was concerned about the conditions that I saw at the zoo and she handed me a business card, circling the number at the bottom of it and telling me I could call in the morning.

That next morning, I did just that, waiting patiently until it was two minutes past nine. The same woman answered.

"It's a wildly exciting summer at the Sacramento Zoo," she said cheerfully. "How can I help you?"

"Hi. I think we talked yesterday," I said. "I'm concerned about the conditions I saw there, and I would like to speak with Nancy Knight."

Her tone changed when she heard it was me. "As I told you yesterday, Nancy is only available by appointment. I'm looking at her calendar, and she is not available until the middle of the next month."

I didn't like how she was talking to me and I definitely didn't like that she had told me to call and now she was telling me that Nancy couldn't talk for a month and a half.

I raised my voice to meet hers. "I need to speak with someone today!"

"I'll see what I can do," she said and asked for my number.

———

My mom and dad had already left for work that morning, so I had the whole house to myself until the late afternoon when my dad would get home. I didn't even think about Nickelodeon. I had a full day to work on my new project. I finished breakfast, showered, and got ready like I was going to school; I had a job to do! Sitting at the kitchen table I finished the last two chapters of *Kids Can Save the Animals*. There was an invitation from the author, who was also the founder of People for the Ethical Treatment of Animals.

"If you would like detailed information on any topic in this book, please do not hesitate to write to me personally," she wrote. "We have fact sheets, cookbooks, leaflets, and we can connect you with the many wonderful organizations who are helping animals."

I decided writing would take too long so I called the operator and got the number to PETA's headquarters in Washington, DC. I was transferred to a woman who was in charge of the international grassroots campaigns, a team at PETA who helped connect local activists with resources. She gave me the names and numbers of two activists who lived in Sacramento and she also promised to send me a package that she thought would be helpful. It was really nice to talk with an adult who cared about animals as much as I did. I felt connected with a community for the first time and I was excited to meet more people who lived close by. Doris was the first person I called because she supposedly knew every animal activist in Northern California. I rang her and she seemed really happy that I called. I opened up immediately and told her all about my family, the bullies at school, and my new-found activism. She was a good listener and even a better talker. She told me about her pack of rescued dogs, about the animal rights phone tree she organized, about the government bugging her house, and about how things had changed for activists in Sacramento.

"Sacramento used to have a big animal activist community," she explained. "But it's just banner drops and visits from PETA these days. There are barely any activists left in our area since the fires at the UC Davis animal research lab ten years ago. The FBI's witch hunts scared everyone out of town."

When I told her I was concerned about the conditions at the zoo, she asked if I knew about the Animal Liberation Front. "They rescue animals from laboratories and farms to send them to better places," she said. "They'll also destroy property that supports the abuse of animals."

"Are you part of the Animal Liberation Front?" I asked her.

"No. I *was* part of a group that communicated to the media about ALF's actions, but we didn't break the law. We were just trying to help the public understand their stance."

I was struggling to understand what Doris was saying. "The Animal Liberation Front breaks the law?"

"Well, yes." Doris slowed down to explain. "It operates on the principle that has been used by every abolitionist movement in history: that property is not a sacred thing if it is used to hurt, destroy, or imprison."

What I was hearing was all so new and exciting. Doris trusted me with her story and treated me like an adult and a friend. She told me I could call her night or day and gave me the numbers to a few activists she thought I might like. I called each of them after we hung up. They all had such good stories and advice for me, but Watson, who had an organization in the Bay Area, was the most interesting character. He was an ex-cowboy who was a vegan and super anti-rodeo. He promised to send me his monthly newsletter in the mail and gave me the phone number of Suzanne, who ran the National Council for Excellence in Zoo Animal Management.

"She is more into animal welfare than she is into animal rights," he warned in his southern drawl. "But if you care about helping zoo animals, she's your lady."

As I went to pick up the phone to call Suzanne, it rang. It was Mom and she sounded pissed. "Justin, what are you doing?" she demanded.

"Nothing," I said.

"I have been trying to call you for the last three hours. Who have you been talking to?"

"Oh…I've been calling people and talking to them about animal rights." I thought she would be proud of me. She wasn't.

"Justin, anything beyond the river is twenty-five cents a minute. Where have you been calling?"

"Just Washington, DC, San Francisco, and some people here in Sacramento."

Making a call could cost up to one dollar a minute depending on when and where I was calling, so she told me to stop using the phone until she and my dad could talk. I agreed and hung up. I was just trying to help animals and all she could think of was how much money I was spending on long-distance phone calls? Would she rather me be outside dying of heat stroke and getting bloodied by the neighbors? The only thing I could think of doing was to make a snack. I toasted a bagel, smothered it in margarine, and dipped it into a perfect mixture of sugar and cinnamon. It was the one sweet thing in our house. I took a bite and then another. I couldn't stop thinking about my mom. *Of course,* she would kill my buzz. *Of course,* she would force me to stop using the phone.

The phone rang, and I jumped. I debated whether it was Mom again with a long list of chores that I needed to have done before she got home. I definitely didn't want to hear that! On the fifth ring, I decided it might not be her, and snatched it up. It was the voice of an unfamiliar man.

"My name is Tim Long. I'm the curator here at the Sacramento Zoo. I hear you have a concern about something."

"Yes. I was at the zoo yesterday and saw a few things that really disturbed me. I was hoping to talk with Nancy Knight and set up a tour to see what's happening behind the scenes there."

"Nancy is busy, so you got me. How old are you anyway?" Tim asked.

"I'm thirteen," I said proudly.

"Well, there's your answer! There's no way we can give you a behind-the-scenes tour of the zoo. Our insurance just wouldn't allow it, plus we are too understaffed for something like that. I assure you that we take excellent care of our animals. You have nothing to worry about."

He spoke to me in a condescending voice I really didn't like. He sounded like he could be the dad of a bully at school, like he would think nothing of pushing me out of the way if he saw me in the hall. "I would really like to talk with Nancy Knight," I said.

He chuckled. "Good luck, kid!"

His laugh and the click of the phone hanging up set something off in me. I couldn't help but ignore my mom's silly rules. I figured I had at least a month before she would see the phone bills, and I decided to call Suzanne. She ran the National Council for Excellence in Zoo Animal Management, volunteered at the Oakland Zoo (which she thought was one of the best in the country), and fought to improve conditions for the animals at the San Francisco Zoo (which she called "third world"). She was really happy to hear that I was investigating the Sacramento Zoo. She explained a lot of things about the zoo industry and had some great information for me about the Sacramento Zoo, most interestingly that the city owned the zoo and that management answered to the city council.

I called Jimmie Yee, the councilman who represented the district where the zoo was located. I didn't just call once, I called and talked to his staff every day for two weeks until I got a call from Nancy Knight. Somehow the zoo's insurance started allowing kids behind the scenes and she found time on her calendar to give me a tour. I realized then that adults lie, city officials can help get things done, and that persistence pays off.

A few days later, Nancy met me at the exact spot she promised over the phone—in front of the turnstiles at ten a.m. She wore khaki shorts, a neatly tucked polo, and a braided belt, and she had a big graying perm. She led me through the zoo past a small aviary with talkative green lorikeets, by a baboon showing off his inflamed red butt, and toward a small cage with two lemurs who bounded our way.

"They seem really excited to see us," I said

"Well, I was the primate keeper for five years before I was director, so these girls know me well."

"Where are they from?" I asked, curious about their native home.

"These two are on loan from Cincinnati." She pointed to the two black-and-white lemurs holding on to the chain link in front of us. "They are part of the species survival plan."

"Wow. So that means that her babies will be released back into the wild?" I asked, thinking that species survival meant survival in the wild.

"Her babies stay here until they are old enough. We don't release animals into the wild, but they'll get transferred to another zoo," Nancy explained before changing the subject. "Shall we grab some carrots and go feed the giraffes?"

Nancy was perfectly nice, but there was something about her I didn't trust. I couldn't tell if she hated me or if she was just putting on a friendly face because she was forced to. Either way, I had a hunch that the best thing to do was to thank her for the tour and keep digging.

Suzanne had told me about the Freedom of Information Act, which allows anyone to request information from the government—an important fact because zoos are regularly inspected by the USDA. I sent a letter requesting any and all records the government had on the Sacramento Zoo. As I placed that letter in the mailbox I felt as if a real investigation was underway.

An overstuffed manila envelope arrived a few days later, revealing a little more: feral cats were killing endangered waterfowl, there was a rat problem in the hornbill exhibit, a broken exterior fence, and there were concerns about quarantine facilities.

"Honey, tacos are ready," my mom screamed from the kitchen.

Since I went vegetarian, frozen Gardenburgers had become a staple and the center of most meals, cooked and crumbled to replace ground beef. I loved taco night! I only wished my dad would stop eating meat and go vegetarian with me and Mom. I made my taco and sat down at the dinner table with my parents.

"Your dad and I talked, and we want you to know we are really proud of the work you're doing," Mom said, and glanced in my dad's direction as she took a bite of her overstuffed taco.

He picked up her thread: "We decided you can use the phone, you just need to be easy on how many calls you're making and be quick with the long-distance ones."

I nodded and thanked them. What a relief! But in the next moment, I felt irritated that Dad was eating meat. It made me feel as if he really didn't care about what I was doing.

"Why can't you just eat the veggie burgers like me and Mom?" I blurted.

"Justin," Dad said, "I'm supporting your choices. You have to respect mine."

"Choice? Let's talk about choice! That cow didn't have a choice to be in your taco."

My dad glared at me. "New house rule. No quoting PETA at the dinner table."

"That mince had a mother *and* eyes," I exclaimed.

"Justin. Listen to your dad," Mom growled.

I shut my mouth because I needed Dad to take me to the zoo the next day. I figured that Nancy had shown me all that she was going to, that I had all of the governmental records I was going to get, and that if I really wanted to help the animals at the zoo, what I really needed was to find someone to give me the inside scoop.

3

I walked through the turnstiles of the zoo with
a new determination. It was 104 degrees outside, and I
didn't want to spend the entire day in that heat, so there
was an urgency to my step. I walked quickly around the
zoo, trying to stay in the shade and find any zookeeper
who might talk. I had done a full circle, hoping to find
the keeper who had led me to Nancy; her nod of support
made me think she might have something more to say. I
lingered around the cluster of cages where I originally saw
her, but she never showed. I didn't see any employees until
I passed through the cactus garden at the front of the
zoo, where I noticed a man in all khakis pushing a plastic wheelbarrow through the side entrance of the reptile

house. I approached the door he left ajar and slipped in behind him.

"Hellllllo?" My voice echoed through the aging concrete building.

"Jesus," the man said. "You scared me, kid. What's going on?"

"I've been researching the zoo and I'm wondering if you can help me."

"Come inside," he said. "I have a bunch to do." We wandered into the dim, humid building. The halls were at least thirty degrees cooler than outside and echoed with the chirps of a thousand crickets. Nancy hadn't taken me there and I couldn't believe I was inside the reptile house, let alone locking eyes with a pit viper that was separated from me only by a wall of thin plastic. I never liked snakes, spiders, or anything that slithered. We scooted past a glass cage with a scary-large Burmese python emerging from a small pool. The thing could have eaten me whole. There were plastic tanks of tarantulas stacked on top of each other and the odor of overfilled mice cages—a terrible mix of urine, poop, and wet fur— made me want to run.

"What are you researching?" the man asked loudly over the feeder crickets.

"I'm concerned about conditions here," I said softly, worried someone might hear me.

"Well, you should be."

My face must have revealed how surprised I was by his words—and how loudly he responded—because he said, "It's just you, me, and the snakes in here. I've been at this place for a long time, and I've seen management come and go. I never liked any of them. Not a single one."

He sounded really bitter and I prodded him to continue. "Why?"

"Where do I begin?" He rolled his eyes. "How about our Yosemite toads? I told Nancy that they wouldn't survive here, but she insisted they'd be a good news story. All twenty of them—one by one—have died. She's an idiot." He poured five small goldfish into the pool of two striped-neck turtles.

"A keeper friend of mine was just telling me about Eloise yesterday—"

"Wait," I said. "Who is Eloise?"

"Eloise *was* a fishing cat." He snapped open the lid of a sand-filled tank covered with rocks and a bright heating lamp. A black scorpion emerged. I took two steps back and bumped something that erupted into a terrifying sound. He spun around. "Be careful. That's our diamond-back. She's off exhibit because she keeps striking at the glass." He shook a bag of crickets into the scorpion cage and snapped it closed. I tried to remember to breathe. I was totally freaked out.

"Eloise was killed by her mate," he said. "She's just one of many that the zoo's bosses could care less about."

I grabbed my notebook from my back pocket and started to write. "Her mate killed her? How did he do that? How did they let that happen?"

"Lea, that's my zookeeper friend, she told the director that the male fishing cat was being particularly aggressive, and asked to stay overnight to monitor Eloise's reintroduction to the exhibit, but Nancy said no because it would mean overtime pay. The male cat killed Eloise that night. Dead. Like Jane, Bruno, my toads, those swans, and so many other animals here."

I was feverishly writing what I was hearing: "Bruno... Jane...Swans."

"Do you think Lea would talk with me?" I asked.

"She's pretty private. Let me ask her. Why don't you give me your number?"

I wrote our house phone number down in my

notepad, ripped the page out, and handed it to him. He stuffed it into the cargo pocket of his shorts, walked over to the fridge, grabbed an old coffee can, and offered it to me. "Would you like to feed the iguanas some mealworms?"

I had no interest in feeding anything in that place and declined, thanking him for the tour.

I walked out of the reptile house, looked around to make sure no one saw me, and snuck onto a gravel path in the cactus garden for cover. I had never been so happy in one hundred degree temperatures. I was grateful to have survived my close encounter with a rattlesnake and a viper, and happy that my visits to the zoo were paying off. As I waited for my dad to pick me up, I thought about all the people who I had connected with over the last month, all the horrific things I had learned about the zoo industry, and all the days I'd spent staring in the mirror and dreaming of being a reporter on TV.

I imagined where I would stand in front of the zoo with my cameraman and what I would say in my live shot. "I am here in front of the Sacramento Zoo, where management is under scrutiny tonight after staff members have criticized the zoo's treatment of animals."

Then I thought a protest might be more effective. I imagined activists surrounding the front entrance of the Sacramento Zoo. Some holding signs saying, *"Polar bears don't belong in 110 degrees."* Others chanting, "The hyena isn't laughing." I visualized the oversized easels with infographics that would block the snack bar. People handing out flyers. Me taunting the passing traffic with a bull horn: "Give the cheetahs a running start!"

The next morning as my parents left for work, the phone rang. I dashed towards the kitchen and picked it up, thinking it might be Lea. It was a woman's voice and she explained that the reptile keeper had given her my number and that both he and Lea had asked her to call. She explained that she was the union representative for the zookeepers and wanted to know a little more about what I was doing. After I explained my goals, she praised my efforts and warned me that I needed to be careful. She had nothing nice to say about the zoo management and she pleaded with me to make sure I protected the keepers' identities. She warned me that their livelihoods were at stake if I didn't. I promised her that I would keep all of my sources anonymous. I had heard the line on an episode of *Murphy Brown* and I figured it might settle her nerves.

A little less than an hour later the phone rang again. It was Lea. Despite my promise to the union rep, Lea didn't sound too sure about me or my intentions.

"You have to understand. The reptile keeper you talked to and I are part of a small group of staff that management despises. We always put animals first and so are always at odds with Nancy and her little cronies."

"The reptile guy was telling me there are a lot of animals who have died recently," I said. "Can you tell me what's happening?"

"Listen. Before I start revealing anything, I need a promise from you. If Nancy ever finds out we are talking, I could be fired. Will you agree to never utter my name to anyone?"

"Absolutely," I said. I was twirling the phone cord around my finger in nervousness. No one had ever told me a real secret. This was serious, and maybe the most grown-up thing I had ever done. "You can trust me," I continued. "All my sources are kept anonymous."

"Okay. This is what I can do for you. I can help you write a letter so that you have all the facts correct about what's going on with the zoo, but you have to write the first draft. I'll read it and will help you rewrite it. Okay?"

I agreed and before we hung up she said one last thing. "I've been impressed with how many times you've visited the zoo. Ever since I first saw you taking notes at the hippo tank and you caught my attention when I was cleaning the lemur cage, I knew you were up to something."

It was her! Lea was the woman who had helped me find Nancy. My hunch that she was on my side was right.

I spent the afternoon in our upstairs loft typing the letter on our oversized, tan Apple Macintosh.

To Whom It May Concern:

Animals kept in the Sacramento Zoo are being denied everything that brings meaning to their lives.

The zoo's polar bear, hyena, cheetahs, and other animals are living in conditions so far removed from their natural environment. They are housed in cages that don't come close to resembling the jungles, savannah, and forests that are their natural homes.

The polar bears and hyenas are housed in unsuitable concrete enclosures. Calling this an educational experience is not only laughable, it's also a lie.

How can you make them live like this? What have these animals done to be put in this prison?

The fifteen acres you have is just too small for
these majestic beings. Please consider eliminating all of
your big animal exhibits.

I called Doris to read her the letter and she had a surprise for me. The Animal Protection Institute had heard about what I was doing and invited me to come work out of extra office space at their headquarters. Not only did I have a mission at Sacramento Zoo, I also had a place to work.

My dad started taking me to API on his way to work every day. It was a shabby old building and my office felt more like a converted storage space. It was stacked tall with chairs and old office equipment. The laminate of my pressed-wood desk was peeling away, and the number three hardly worked on my phone—but I had a desk and a place to make free long-distance calls. API had a bustling staff of thirty and almost as many dogs. The sounds of clacking keyboards and the repetitious greetings from the receptionist answering the phone were mixed with the panting and the odd squabbles of canines.

Everything began coming together—and quickly. Lea called my first draft "overly emotional and poorly written" but over five more calls she helped me rewrite it, and the final draft was explosive—revealing a long list of abuses she had witnessed at the zoo. "Things no one knows about," Lea promised. I shared the letter with Suzanne, who had been advising me about zoo politics, and she happened to know the lead inspector for the American Zoo and Aquarium Association. The association held zoos to a certain standard and Sacramento Zoo happened to be up for an inspection that month, something that only happened every five years. She promised to share my letter with the lead inspector.

The timing of everything couldn't have been more perfect. It was so perfect that I couldn't help but think about life and why I was here—how at thirteen years old I had my own office and in a matter of six weeks had built up a network of people all over the country on whom I could call. I felt like all of this had to be more than luck or just being in the right place at the right time. The way things were falling into place felt much bigger than me, almost divine. It felt like something that was completely meant to be. How did that book stand out the way it did at the bookstore? What drew me to the Sacramento Zoo? How on earth did I end up at the reptile house that day? What were the chances that I would meet the two zookeepers who would reveal the inner chaos and agree to talk to me about the zoo?

Lea didn't think the AZA would actually hold the zoo accountable, because the organization's core mission was to ship baby animals all over the country. I set up a meeting with the executive director of the Animal Protection Institute, hoping he might be able to help me and possibly bring the story to the media—something my book had often talked about.

He had a spacious corner office full of large houseplants and an oversized glass desk that dominated the space. I had seen him in passing but we never really talked. I thanked him for letting me use their offices for the summer and described what I had learned about the zoo. He thought he could help me, explaining he knew a reporter at the *Sacramento Bee* who loved animals. A week later, both my zookeeper friends met with the executive director in the privacy of the institute's dusty basement library to corroborate everything I had shared with him in the letter.

Late July sun streamed into my closet when my mom slid the door open. "Honey, wake up, wake up," she said. She was holding the *Sacramento Bee* in her hands and held the front page up for me to see. As my eyes adjusted to the brightness of the day, I saw a large photo of the zoo's lone hyena and then I read the headline: "Zoo Fails Accreditation Review."

"Oh my God," I said. I scrambled out of my closet and grabbed the paper from her. "It's happening, Mom."

My mom had mixed feelings about the whole thing. She loved that I had found something that I was passionate about, was sickened by everything she heard about at the zoo, but she thought the zookeepers were real cowards for making me do their dirty work. Because of this, I hadn't really told her about the details of my work—until it landed on the front page of the paper. "The letter that Lea helped me write was forwarded to the AZA inspection committee by Suzanne," I said. "She knows the committee head, and it looks like he read the letter." I was out of breath from excitement.

"Let's have breakfast," Mom said, "and I can read us the article."

Mom made oatmeal topped with brown sugar and read the piece out loud:

Inspectors said the zoo's polar bears and hyenas were both housed in unsuitable concrete enclosures and team members questioned the fact that the zoo still housed polar bears, given, among other issues, Sacramento's summer heat. They also said the gibbons, foxes, lemurs, and fishing cat are housed in cages that are too small.

"Yeees! That is a direct quote from my letter! I have to call Suzanne and Doris and get to API. Mom, can you take me there in an hour?"

I explained the whole story to my mom on the way to API. She dropped me off and I went running up the stairs through the front door towards the executive director's office. I busted in without knocking and threw the newspaper onto his desk. "It's happening. The accreditation was suspended, and they used an exact quote from my letter. Check it out."

He didn't seem pleased with my barging in, but I could have cared less; this moment was far too important for office etiquette. He was happy about the article and told me the reporter he knew was working on a follow-up story about the abuse claims.

One week to the day after the failed accreditation story broke, I woke up to another front-page article, this time with a large photo of the zoo's overheating polar bear snuggling a block of ice and the headline: "Zoo's Care of Animals Criticized."

"Mooom, Daaad. There is another article in the *Bee*." I hooted.

While the Sacramento Zoo was putting the finishing touches on its two-million-dollar Lake Victoria exhibit, Bruno the grizzly bear was slowly dying—staggering and bleeding in his concrete enclosure in full view of the public several days before a veterinarian was called to end his agony.

The article went on to expose Eloise's death, Jane the nyala's tragic end, and the fate of those twenty Yosemite toads—quoting zookeepers and the director of API.

This is a very serious issue, and Sacramento should be embarrassed. It is the zoo's responsibility to take care of the animals, and in that it has failed.

It was unbelievable that by asking the right questions, working hard, and insisting that people pay attention I could actually have an impact in the world—and in only a matter of months. I was mesmerized by the power of speaking up and by the work I had done for animals at the zoo. That a single letter could influence a national organization and my investigative work could end up on the front page of the paper was mind-blowing. That night Dad, Mom, and I sat down to watch the news. We flipped through each channel until we landed on KOVR 13. Every top story that night was about the zoo's neglect. My dreams of colorful protests seemed almost unnecessary. The battle was being waged over the airwaves, and, sitting there with my parents, I had a terrible thought: with eighth grade fast approaching, my free time would disappear, and my activism would have to slow down.

The city scrambled to respond to the zoo's accreditation suspension and the accusations of neglect. Within a few weeks they announced they would establish an exploratory committee to address the problems the zoo faced and that they would invite two citizens to join. I figured I was the perfect fit for the role and called Nancy to offer my services.

"What do you want, Justin?" She was angry.

"I'm ready to join the exploratory committee to improve the zoo. I have some great ideas."

"Look, Justin," she said sternly. "You have caused a lot of problems for me and the animals here. I will tell you right now: if you continue defaming me and the zoo, you are going to be sued. What you have done is called slander and it's illegal. Stop harassing me and stop calling the AZA complaining about me."

My heart raced and my breath shortened. Her tone scared me. I had never heard the word "slander", let alone been threatened with a lawsuit.

That night, I walked into the kitchen as Dad emptied a bag of frozen cheese-and-spinach ravioli into a pot of boiling water while my mom sliced chunks of avocado into a heaping bowl of salad. It was clear what was for dinner, but I asked anyway. My mom looked up.

"Are you okay, Justin?" She could tell by my voice that I was not.

"Well...I just got off the phone with Nancy Knight and she told me she was going to sue me for slander."

I had my parents' attention. "Why would she say that?" Mom asked.

"She told me that I slandered her name."

My dad cut in. "Is that true?"

"No. I've been honest about what's happening at the zoo and everything is verified by the keepers."

"Those cowards." Mom shook her head.

Dinner was somber that night. "Look, Justin," Dad explained. "There's no way that Nancy Knight can sue you. You're only thirteen years old. But she can very well sue *us*. We don't really know what you are getting up to, but we can't afford to be sued."

"Mom *knows* what I'm doing."

"Honey. You are doing good work. We are proud of you, but this zoo project has turned really negative," Mom said softly. "We can't afford to be sued."

"What's negative about it? The AZA just tabled the zoo's accreditation, the *Bee* just exposed animal abuse—"

"—and the zoo director just threatened to sue you." Dad finished my sentence. "Aren't you at all scared about that?"

"I'm a little scared, but the zoo animals need me. I need to talk with Doris about it. She has experience with these kinds of things." I got up from the table mid-meal without any of their normal resistance.

"You're doing dishes tonight," my mom called out as I dialed Doris's number and pulled the long cord into my room.

"There is *no* way she can sue you or your parents,"

Doris said. She was irate. "That is absurd. Hasn't she ever heard of free speech? Jesus!"

"Thanks, Doris. One thing before I go.....Next week is a big council meeting about the zoo. Could you put it in this week's phone tree? We need some animal rights people there that night. It's Wednesday at six p.m."

I went back to the kitchen where my parents were still sitting at the dinner table, empty plates in front of them. "Doris told me that we have nothing to worry about. Nancy is just trying to scare me."

Dad spoke up. "Your mom and I were talking. We think that it's time you find a new project. You're in over your head with this zoo. You have already done a lot to help the animals."

"Noooo. Pleeease," I cried. I was desperate. "I'm starting school soon. I won't have much time to work on it anyway." I realized my parents could end it all right there and I figured I had to do one last thing if their request was real. "Could you at least take me to the city council meeting on Wednesday? It is really important! Then I will find a new project. I promise." They agreed.

That following Wednesday evening my dad took me to the council meeting. We walked up the marble steps of city hall. It was a beautiful building with a traditional dome and roman-like pillars, all surrounded by a big expansive lawn and large elm trees that emitted a pungent smell in the summer. The zoo was the main agenda item that evening. We walked through the doors of the city hall. "What are you going to say tonight?" my dad asked.

"I'm just going to speak from my heart," I said.

He sat on a wooden bench in front of an old TV screen with a feed from the council chambers. "Dad. What are you doing?"

"Buddy, you go do your thing in there. I will watch out here."

I opened the chamber doors to a packed and loud audience. Almost every seat was taken, and it looked like everyone was there for the same reason. Zookeepers, docents, and volunteers in bright orange polos seemed to make up most of the audience.

There was a small group of familiar faces—all gray-haired ladies from the animal rights community. I waved to them but decided to sit with the keepers' union representative. We had talked that week about everything that had unfolded, and she had promised to save me a seat. The room was loud, and the energy was intense. I settled in next to her and a former docent from the zoo I had never met. I leaned over to the union representative. "I'm a little nervous," I said.

I saw Nancy a few rows up, surrounded by zoo staff. A woman sitting next to her looked over her shoulder and saw me with the union rep. The look in her eyes scared me. "Oh God," the rep said under her breath, as the very large woman got up from her seat and stormed towards the back of the room, straight for us. She was almost three hundred pounds with auburn hair that reached her lower back. The tag on her ill-fitting polo shirt read: "Lead Keeper." I was warned about her; she was Nancy's right-hand lady.

"You're so unprofessional," she said, spit flying in our direction as she pointed at the union rep's face. "I can't believe you're sitting with this punk. You're supposed to be representing the keepers, not creating alliances with animal activists. Unbelievable." Her eye twitched as she glared at us. The chamber was loud enough that no one really noticed the exchange except Nancy, who had turned her head enough to witness it. She had a smirk on her face.

"Order in the chamber. Order" The city manager quieted the room as six council members and the mayor settled into the semicircle of seats slightly elevated above the crowd.

The mayor sat smack-dab in the middle of it all in a brown leather executive chair. He was a charismatic and celebrated leader with community organizing roots. His broad shoulders and perfect hair matched his personality. "It looks like a lot of you are here for our big item this evening regarding the zoo. If you look at this evening's agenda, you'll see that the zoo is the last item. We want to make time to hear all of your comments so please be patient and keep them short."

The council went on for hours discussing everything from a new baseball field downtown to a proposed change to the city's scavenging laws. It was nine p.m. by the time the agenda item that everyone was waiting for was called, and the long meeting had tired everyone out.

The mayor invited Nancy to address the council. She was in pressed khakis and a forest-green polo, sitting at a desk to the right of a large podium where the public had aired their grievances all evening. Nancy's speech to the council mainly focused on budgetary concerns and proposed a change to the structure of the zoo.

"We propose the city would retain ownership of the zoo and would turn management over to the Sacramento Zoological Society. I know we could run the facility in a more entrepreneurial way."

Jimmie Yee, the councilmen who helped me get my first meeting with Nancy, raised his hand. "Could you give us some examples of what that might look like?"

"Sure. We imagine selling corporate sponsorships of exhibits and even for our many pathways. Our chimps brought to you by Campbell's Soup. Polar bears brought to you by Shell."

One of the councilwomen interjected. "Could you address the polar bears? The zoo has been in the media lately for all the wrong reasons. This AZA report"—she held up a blue binder—"questions why Sacramento even has polar bears."

Nancy was quick to respond. "Those bears are third-generation bred in captivity and are more adapted to the heat. But they do not match our master plan theme of river animals, so we will most likely be shipping them to another facility."

Council members threw Nancy a bunch of soft-ball questions and seemed satisfied with her mediocre responses. It felt like the same bullshit I had heard time and time again from Nancy.

"We are going to open the mic to the public. We have collected all your requests for comment. We will call your name and will limit you to one minute," the city manager explained.

"Justin Barker," he said. I was the first one?

My heart raced so fast I could feel it in my legs. My vision tunneled as I walked toward the council and up a step to the podium where I adjusted the mic to my mouth.

"Good evening, Council. I'm a thirteen-year-old kid who has been working on improving conditions for the zoo animals in Sacramento." My voice shook with nerves. "There are a lot of problems at the Sacramento Zoo and I think the biggest one is the current management. Just last week Nancy Knight threatened to sue me for slander."

I paused, surprised those words came out of my mouth. There were hisses from the audience. I wasn't sure if they were against what I was saying or against Nancy's threat of a lawsuit.

The mayor looked surprised. "Nancy. Is what this young man is saying true?"

"Yes. I did tell him we would sue him. He's been—"

The mayor interrupted her. "That is a big problem, Nancy." The mayor's voice boomed. "You're a city employee and the only person who should be threatening legal action in this town is the city attorney. Do you understand that?"

Nancy nodded in agreement and I was so nervous I couldn't think of anything more to say.

The rest of the public's comments most likely went on for hours, but I couldn't leave my dad waiting in the hall, so I left.

"I'm really impressed with you," he said, patting my back as we walked toward the car. "It's a big thing getting in front of that many people and speaking your mind."

He started snickering. "Did you see Nancy's face when the mayor called her out?" My dad seemed to have enjoyed the spectacle.

"Everything was a blur to me. I didn't even mean to tell the council about that! I wanted to focus on the animals. But I'm kinda glad I did."

"I'm glad you did, too," Dad said. He looked relieved. We both laughed.

There never was a lawsuit, I was not invited to join the zoo's exploratory committee, and I followed through on my promise to my parents that I would leave my Sacramento Zoo activism behind. It was hard to walk away knowing that Penny would remain pacing in her cage without the sand I knew she pined for; that the cheetahs' sprints would continue to be stunted by chain link; and that the polar bears would have to endure our city's scorching heat. Fall and winter were on the way, so the bears would get a break, but I would soon face the first day of eighth grade and another year of standardized testing, timed miles, and relentless bullying.

I watched as the hands of the science room clock moved to meet at noon, triggering the long drone of the third-period bell. That bell had a totally different meaning for me in eighth grade. It meant it was lunchtime and I had an hour to escape the trivialities that dominated every other second of junior high. I shoved my textbook into my backpack and bolted towards the open door, half running through the quad to avoid the snide comments and to get to the library as quickly as I could. I had discovered that the doughnuts I loved eating for lunch in seventh grade were made with beef fat, so those were out, but I convinced the lunch lady to offer Gardenburgers on the lunch line. She put them next to the regular burgers for a month or so, but no one ate them, and of course, people teased me for them. They would chomp their burgers in my face and tell me veggie burgers were for girls. She pulled the burgers from the lunch line but promised to make one special for me every day. I'd eat it as quickly as possible since there was no food allowed in the library and I needed every minute of that hour-long break.

I decided to expand on my success at the Sacramento Zoo and started investigating all of the zoos in California. On weekends my parents would take me to inspect the zoos near our house. I inspected the LA Zoo on a family road trip. I had spent two lunch periods scribbling potential names for my new project in my binder: Helping Animals in Zoos. Saving Zoo Animals. No More Cages. Citizens Helping Animals in Zoos. Rethinking Zoos. Protect Animals in Zoos. Close the Zoos.

None of them felt right, so I decided to ask the librarian if she had any ideas. We had become friends after I told her about what had happened over the summer at the Sacramento Zoo. She loved that story and had ordered a bunch of animal rights books for the library. I think she also understood that I was one of those kids who had no one else at school to talk to.

I walked up to the counter and she greeted me with her warm smile. I snapped open my binder and handed her the list I had been working on. "Do you like any of these names?"

She looked at the list, then circled around the desk. "Let's sit down and work on them." We sat next to each other at a table and she moved her finger over the long list, pausing quickly at each one.

"What's your favorite?" she asked.

"Close the Zoos is my favorite," I responded.

"I don't know about that one. I think you need an affirmative name. I like Citizens Helping Animals in Zoos. An acronym like PETA could be cool." She spelled out C-H-A-Z. "That's not great," she said, then pondered some ideas and scribbled them on the page. "What about Citizens Lobbying for Animals in Zoos? That would make it CLAZ, like you are clawing through zoos." She curled her fingers scraping the air, showing off her teeth like a tiger. We both laughed.

"And you *are* a zoo animal lobbyist," she said.

"What's a lobbyist?"

"Lobbyists influence decisions in politics and insist on action."

"That is so cool! CLAZ. Citizens Lobbying for Animals in Zoos. That's it!"

The second the last bell rang that day, I darted through the busy halls toward my bike. It was Friday and I couldn't wait to get home. I put my helmet on and raced down the street, knowing there were only two stop lights between me and all the calls I had to make that day. I stood up on my bike almost the entire way, slowing just enough to roll through each stop sign, peddling down the wide sidewalks and under the towering oak trees of the suburbs.

On the days my mom worked, I had four hours before my dad would arrive home. It gave me a chance to focus on my activism without any requests to mow the lawn or complaints about long-distance calls. I always stopped at the big metal mailbox a few houses up from ours. It was one of those oversized units that held mail for fifteen families, with a large compartment for packages. Our small cubby was able to handle all the mail we received until I made that first call to PETA. Ever since then, I would usually open our small mailbox and it would hold another key that would unlock the huge compartment that held many packages, most addressed to me. On that particular day my parents received the phone bill, and I received a monthly magazine from PETA, a small bubble package of bumper stickers and buttons, and the package I was most excited about—a large box that I could hardly fit in my arms. The return address was from the *Shape of Enrichment*, a magazine for zookeepers. I had ordered the entire back catalog. I left my bike parked in front of the mailbox, ran home, set the box on our front doorstep, and raced back to grab my bike. I peddled home as fast as I could, throwing my bike sideways on our lawn. I got inside, grabbed a butter knife, and sliced through the packing tape. Styrofoam peanuts overflowed everywhere.

When Nancy Knight told me that I knew nothing about zoo animals, she was wrong. I knew they were not here for our entertainment. I knew that if they had their way, they would choose freedom. I knew that if I had my way, I would have closed down every zoo. I also knew that it wasn't reasonable to shutter zoos and that if I wanted to truly help animals, I needed to improve their conditions *inside* of zoos. That's why I spent seventy-eight dollars— four months of allowance—for those magazines. The one thing I hated most about zoos was seeing the insanity they induced in animals. Other than expansive exhibits, behavioral enrichment was the easiest thing keepers could do to help animals cope with their boredom and challenges in captivity. I flipped through the binders, scanning articles like "Mealtime Activities for Lemurs," "Olfactory Enrichment for Fruit Bats," and "Wonders for Walruses." I landed on an article called "New World Primate Enrichment," reading about techniques to keep small primates busy throughout the day, just like they are in the wild.

I was determined to read the hundreds of articles these volumes held, not just to understand the plight of zoo animals, but to have a solution for the people that kept them. I figured if I spotted an animal pacing, over-grooming, or other signs of stress, I was only a photocopy away from helping ease their pain.

My room had become my office and the headquarters for CLAZ and I was so happy to add this bundle of knowledge to my collection. I had collected hundreds of fact sheets, pamphlets, buttons, and bumper stickers about animal rights.

I listed all my contact information in a few animal rights directories and almost immediately started fielding correspondence. One day I got a call from the chimpanzee keepers at Marine World Africa USA, an amusement park an hour from my house. They were a husband-and-wife team who had cared for a family of seven chimpanzees for thirteen years.

"They canceled our show and they are breaking up the family," she sobbed.

"They are sending the babies to Florida and they have no idea what to do with the adults." She begged for my help. I sat at my desk, just listening to her, and apologized for the terrible news. I recommended she contact the media, which she did. There wasn't much more I could do, but her call made me realize how important my work for zoo animals was. The bonds those chimps built with each other and their human companions meant nothing to the management. It was clear that many people thought it was okay to treat animals like commodities.

I was one of those kids who could only focus if my surroundings were impeccably clean, so everything had to have its place. My speckled white walls were covered in perfectly straight posters, the biggest one being of Elizabeth Berkley, an actress who starred in *Saved by the Bell*. She wore a dress made of collard greens. The poster said, "Let Vegetarianism Grow on You." Another said, "We'd Rather Go Naked Than Wear Fur," with a lineup of Naomi Campbell and other supermodels sitting naked, perfectly cross-legged to cover their own fur.

I had a large oak desk with a paper blotter for note taking, two mesh trays to manage incoming and outgoing mail, a matching pen holder, and a Rolodex. Long before smartphones, the best way to organize your contacts was with one of these devices. It was a kind of circular card file you could flip around to access people's contact information. Mine had a transparent plastic top and sat flush with the right corner of my desk when I wasn't using it. It held at least a hundred contacts written on index cards and organized alphabetically. It became one of my prized possessions. It helped me access people around the world and reminded me that I was only a flip away from a friendly voice of someone who cared about animals as much as I did.

My Rolodex wasn't the only thing that I alphabetized. I also had two large plastic boxes filled with hanging files that held every piece of literature and mail I had received. The first box focused on general animal rights broken down by topic, and the second held all the articles, inspection reports, research papers, and correspondence about zoos I was investigating. With the arrival of my new magazines and the endless onslaught of packages that continued to arrive every week, I soon needed a third and fourth box. I also needed a fax machine—another high-tech item that let you send and receive hard copies of papers, like a hard copy of an emailed pdf today. It was the one thing I wanted for my fourteenth birthday.

My perfectly kept office masked the chaos and confusion that swirled in my teenage brain. With my parents bearing the brunt of my hormonal storm, I wondered if I would get anything at all for my birthday that year. Our relationships had improved over the summer when Nancy Knight was the one in my crosshairs, but with the start of school, we all returned to our old ways. My weekly fights with my dad and mom had returned. She had ramped up her threats and followed through on abusively long restrictions. My dad's backbone continued to shrink; he was unwilling to speak up against her unreasonable ways. I locked him out of the house one day and he somehow had enough of a spine to call the police on me. After that, my parents insisted I go to a therapist for help. I didn't think I was the only one who needed counseling, but I agreed to go. I hated the way we treated each other, and I was also sick of the restrictions. I had work I needed to do and whenever I was cut off from the phone, it all came to a halt. I just hoped the therapist would be on my side.

My mom looked desperate when she dropped me off for my first appointment, insisting we'd find the right therapist if this one wasn't the one. I shrugged and went in. The office was full of stuffed animals, games, and a punching bag. The therapist asked me to arrange a group of toy dinosaurs in a sand pit and then tried to interpret the arrangement, telling me I was the Brachiosaurus who had turned my back on the world. I interpreted her as crazy and never returned. The second therapist had me close my eyes and visualize a warm, safe place. I imagined never lying on her couch again.

I returned to my bedroom office to keep doing my work, but the tension was always there. One day I was filing away the day's mail when I heard the front door open. My mom was home. It must have been her day off. She yelled for my help. I went running into the kitchen, not to help her but to grab the phone bill before she could see it. Her arms were hugging two grocery bags when she intercepted me in the doorway of the kitchen. That month's phone bill sat partially covered by a few other envelopes addressed to my parents and a few packages addressed to me.

"What's all of this?" she asked, setting the paper bags on the counter.

All I could think of was the phone bill. "It's nothing! What, what do you mean?"

"What do you mean it's nothing?" she said, pointing to the bubble wrap and a pile of packing peanuts on the counter.

"Oh. That!" I chuckled nervously. "I got a few packages from PETA."

With the squint of her eyes, I knew she knew I was up to something.

"Go grab the last bag in the car. The ice cream is in there."

My mom always made me whatever I asked for on my birthday and that year it was pecan pie with vanilla ice cream. I lingered, hoping she would turn her back, but she just stared at me.

"Go. It's melting," she urged, and I jogged toward the front door.

When I walked back in and set the grocery bag down, my mom was shuffling through the mail. She knew the phone bill had arrived, so there was nothing I could do. "Clean this mess up so I can start baking," she insisted.

I cupped the peanuts back into the box, took it out to the trash, and thought about all the options that might unfold that evening once they saw the phone bill. Maybe my parents would be easy on me because it was my birthday, maybe the bill wasn't that bad this month, maybe it was worse than usual and I should just run away. I could sneak back in through my window to sleep at night.

I told my mom I was going to work on my homework. I retreated to my room and did something I rarely did—prayed to God.

He didn't hear me.

"JUUUUUUUSTIN!" My mom screamed so loud our windows probably shook. "Get out here now."

I went from frightened and hiding away, to angry and irritated. I charged into the living room where she sat. "Don't yell at me like that. I'm not deaf."

"Clearly not! The phone bill this month is three hundred and fifty dollars!"

I was surprised by the amount but was defensive. "All you care about is money! You don't care that I'm helping animals or anything else."

"Bring me your Rolodex," she insisted.

"No," I said.

"Go get it now. You can't use the phone until you've paid this bill." Her lip quivered.

I got thirty dollars a month in allowance and did a quick calculation. It would take me almost a year before I could use the phone again. I had had it. "You're fucking crazy," I said.

"Get in your room now and if you say the F word one more time—"

"FUCK YOU," I yelled.

I went running into the kitchen, opened the fridge, and grabbed the pie she had just finished. It smelled amazing. She came in after me just in time to catch me scooping the entire midsection into my hand and shoving it into the sink. I flipped on the garbage disposal. She turned around and went toward my room. I thought she was going for my phone numbers, so I followed her. Instead, she unclicked the lid to the box of file folders and flung its contents across my room. Paper flew in all directions.

"What are you doing?" I asked in disbelief.

She grabbed the second box and did the same thing. "You trash my work, I trash yours." She snagged my Rolodex and walked out of my room, slamming my door behind her. I burst into tears.

I picked up the papers, one by one, and stacked them on my bed, my tears smearing the ink. I usually called Doris after a fight, but I didn't have her number and I could faintly make out my mom talking on the phone, telling someone about our fight.

———

I walked into the kitchen the next morning—it was a Saturday—to my mom and dad sitting at the table and drinking coffee. I was sure my mom would apologize for trashing my office, but instead, they sat me down and told me that they had found a therapist who worked on weekends and that we were all going to go to her. "You'll go for an hour to talk with her first and then we will join you after," my dad explained.

A few hours later we all pulled into the driveway of a small house in a cul-de-sac in the Fabulous 40s, an upscale neighborhood in Sacramento. My parents walked me up the driveway, past clothes hanging on a line, up to a door that read "Dr. Sybil Newton." I figured she was just another new-age crystal lover who would try to chant or visualize our problems away. My dad knocked, and a voice welcomed us in. We walked into a small, dark room that smelled like cooking.

"You must be Justin," Sybil said with a smile as she struggled to push her weight out of the chair she was sitting in. She wore a floral housedress that draped over her large body. She greeted my parents and asked them to return in an hour. Between her chair and the large leather couch she welcomed me to sit in was a messy coffee table stacked with newspapers, opened mail, and an old phone. Her walls were covered in tribal masks and other African art. This was like no therapist's office I had been to before, and Sybil was like no therapist. There wasn't any sunlight because her shades were drawn, but she radiated warmth.

"Your mom seems kinda intense," she said, as I settled into the squeaky leather. Despite having to sit on a dead cow, I liked her immediately. She was real and she listened, unlike the uptight white therapists I had seen before. I told her everything that had happened between me and my parents and she explained how things were going to go down when they came back.

"I'm here to help you. If you or your parents are out of line, I'll call you out. Ya dig?"

"Yeah," I responded, happy to hear we would all be held responsible.

"What?" she asked.

"Yeah," I said again.

"What?" she asked, raising her eyebrows. I realized she didn't like my casual response.

"Yes," I said, and she nodded.

"I don't do 'yeahs' or 'yeps.' You hear?"

"Yes," I confirmed.

I had no idea of the impact Sybil would end up having on me and my family's life, but on that first visit she checked my mom's attitude, which was highly entertaining, and even more importantly she helped me get phone privileges back after I agreed to keep long-distance calls to less than five minutes.

I also had no idea of the other ways my life was about to change.

———

A month or so after that first visit with Sybil, we were driving back from an appointment when my dad pulled up to the mailbox. I jumped out to open it, grabbed the stack of mail, and flipped through the letters. One stood out. It was handwritten and addressed to CLAZ. I ripped it open and read it as Dad pulled the minivan into the darkness of our garage.

> *Dear CLAZ,*
>
> *I am writing to your organization because I am desperate.*
>
> *I was told you might be able to help me help two bears who are living in terrible conditions here in Roseville, California.*
>
> *Brutus and Ursula are sibling black bears who are living in a defunct zoo near my house. The zoo*

used to be home to monkeys, a mountain lion, and rabbits, but they were all washed away in floods, leaving only the bears behind. Their cage is not much bigger than a shipping container and has a lone tire swing that Ursula bats and a pool that is too small for Brutus to fit in.

Their cage is next to a creek that floods almost every winter requiring them to be tranquilized and moved to an even smaller cage.

I have wanted to help these bears since I first saw them five years ago, but I don't know what to do.

Can you help?

I learned there are two kinds of adults: ones who believe in kids and ones who don't. I had a whole Rolodex of people who believed in me, so when I called the woman who wrote me about the bears, I was a little surprised by her reaction. She was certain she had written to a well-staffed organization for help and was shocked by my prepubescent voice. I was confident I could actually do something to help the bears and didn't let her negativity get to me; in fact, it felt like a good challenge. I promised her that no matter what it took or how long, I would help the bears. I told her about what I had accomplished at the Sacramento Zoo, the research I had done to understand the needs of captive animals, and all the people I could call for advice, but she was terribly skeptical.

My parents were sitting at the table and had listened to my entire conversation. They were both grinning ear to ear, giddy from the exchange. Things had gotten better between us since we started seeing Sybil regularly. We definitely still fought, but Sybil helped my parents understand my teenage brain, advocated for me, and insisted I work on my diplomacy. One of the things we all knew for sure was if I was focused on a project, we were all better off.

"We knew you'd find your next project," my mom said.

"When are we going to see the bears?" my dad asked.

I couldn't believe how supportive they were being, so I called my dad's bluff. "Can we go right now?" I asked.

"Let's go!" my dad said, looking at my mom for approval.

She nodded. "I'll make dinner and you two take a drive."

I figured their excitement was more about getting a reprieve from my sharp tongue than about helping the bears, but I honestly didn't care what inspired their support. I was just happy to be heading to see the bears.

We drove thirty minutes to Roseville. When we turned off the freeway and headed toward a sea of trees, I saw a large green sign that said, WELCOME TO ROYER PARK,

THE PRIDE OF ROSEVILLE. "Turn here; this is it, this is it," I said.

We drove up a narrow road, past picnic benches and a large playground full of screaming kids, following the directions the letter writer had given me. Royer Park was beautiful with towering old trees and well-maintained lawns. My dad and I drove until the road dead-ended at a crescent-shaped fence that butted up against the edge of a small creek. Beyond that heavy-duty chain-link fence, all the beauty and care vanished, and I witnessed something no human could possibly be proud of. I had never seen such horrible conditions for animals and couldn't believe that two fully grown black bears were indeed living in a cage slightly larger than a forty foot shipping container.

What had been their home for fifteen years was a cage made of wood and thick gauged metal fencing painted a dark green and peeling from years of exposure. Two small, hand-painted signs hung crookedly, facing the public. One read "*Brutus*" and the other "*Ursula*."

There was a lone tire swing, a small water hole covered in muck, and a three-tiered, wooden platform that the bears could climb up. In the back corner, there was a small metal door that lead to a five-by-seven-foot-long brick addition—the only place the bears could escape from view or the elements. The concrete floor was covered in a layer of algae that matched the green tint of the painted cage.

Brutus was lying on the second tier of the wood platform. He hung his big head over the edge, swatting a fly with his paw. My heart sank when I looked into his eyes. Nowhere to go. Nothing to do. If he was in the wild, he would travel up to forty miles a day, sniffing out berries, climbing trees, communicating with his friends, digging up grubs, scratching his back on stumps, and fishing in the river. It seemed fifteen years in that hell hole had completely broken his spirit.

Ursula poked her head out of the brick enclosure and struggled to fit her large body through the small, rusted door of their sleeping quarters. She was much shorter than her brother and much fatter. Ursula began to walk a loop around the interior of their cage, losing her footing on the slimy algae every time she turned a corner. Based on the path worn in the concrete, it looked like she'd made that circuit thousands of times before.

I pressed my arms against the top of the four-foot fence that kept a distance between the bears' cage and the public, leaning in to witness everything I could. While I was sad about what I was seeing, the burning sensation inside of me was overwhelming and I felt so many things. Anger. Rage. Resentment. My jaw clenched. Bears are intelligent, affectionate, and altruistic animals. Clearly the people who thought these conditions were acceptable had none of these traits.

My dad stood next to me and touched my shoulder. "You know, some Miwok believe we descended from bears." He had been telling me about native mythology my entire life. "The Miwok live close to here. They have always been peaceful people who honor the warrior spirit of the bear." I wondered if he could tell that the anger in my body was rising and if it was even possible to be a warrior and peaceful at the same time.

A man emerged from the storage shed adjacent to the cage and lumbered toward us with a big blue bucket. He squeezed through a small gate at the rear of the cage and dumped food pellets through a chute that landed in a puddle of water below. Feeding time got the attention of both of the bears and a rat who poked its head out of a drainage pipe inside the cage and scurried toward the food faster than Ursula could reach it. It grabbed a single pellet in its mouth and darted back into the pipe it came from. Ursula sniffed the pile and filled her mouth with three pellets and plopped herself down to eat.

"Excuse me," I screamed, getting the big man's attention. "What did you just feed them?" I asked, acting like I was a dumb kid.

"It's monkey chow," he responded.

"What else do you feed them?" I shouted back.

"That's it," he said.

The moment I got home from school the next day, I called Performing Animal Welfare Society, an organization that rescued animals from circuses and abusive animal trainers. They told me they fed their bears a mix of omnivore chow, fresh fruit, vegetables, and live fish every week. I hung up and dialed the Roseville mayor's office. Somehow the receptionist gave me the mayor's home phone number.

"Vern Fernsby speaking," he answered, taking an audible gulp of a drink.

I told him my concerns about the bears. Clearly, my call was not the one the mayor had been expecting.

"Those bears?" He chuckled dismissively. "That zoo was part of FDR's New Deal. We have had bears here since the thirties and those two are happy. Our grandkids love seeing them."

Luckily, I had just learned about the New Deal in school. It was a series of federal projects during the 1930s that invested in infrastructure and were meant to get people working again after the Great Depression. "Did you hear what you just said?" I asked him. "Two bears are living in a cage that was built during the Great Depression. How could you say they are happy?"

"Those bears *are* happy." The mayor sounded like he really believed what he was saying.

"The concrete is covered in algae and Ursula slips all over the place," I said. "She has worn a path from her constant pacing and has to battle a rat to eat food that is meant for monkeys. You should be ashamed!"

"Ashamed? Royer Park is the pride of the city! You are the only one to ever complain about those bears."

"I'm not complaining about the bears," I said. "I'm complaining about how the city is treating the bears. I'm asking for—"

The mayor cut me off. "Low priority. Can't help you, kid. My dinner's getting cold."

And then he hung up.

I couldn't believe it—and I knew exactly what to do. If the mayor wouldn't take my call seriously, I thought a little spotlight from the media might get his attention.

If I had learned only one thing during my experience at the Sacramento Zoo, it was about the power of the press. PETA taught me that a good demonstration required a good visual to get some attention, and over that next week, I developed my plan.

I dialed the Roseville newspaper and was transferred to a reporter who was very sympathetic to my concerns about the bears. I told her about my plan to bring a big box of the food the bears *should* be eating, and she agreed to meet me with a photographer the next day. I got off the phone and squealed. I jumped up and down and went running through the house. When I finally settled down, I called a few food distributors, eventually finding one who agreed to donate a box of fruit and some seafood. I couldn't believe how easy it was to get a donation and the attention of a news reporter. My parents were equally impressed at dinner that evening and my mom agreed to pick me up from school and take me to Roseville.

The next day we hurried to the warehouse district to pick up the large box of fruit and crawdads and weaved through rush hour traffic to hit feeding time. A well-dressed woman and man with a large camera were waiting at the bear's cage when we pulled up.

"You must be Justin," the woman said. The big box of fruit in my arms gave me away.

I was a little nervous about the whole thing and gave them a closed-mouth smile, worried they might get a photograph of my crooked teeth and that everyone might see my braces.

"What do you think of when you see the bears in this cage?" she asked.

"I think it should be illegal," I said. "Why have they been subjected to this kind of confinement? What have they done?"

The reporter scribbled in her notepad.

"What's the worst part about it for you?" she prodded.

"The cage is just too small for animals this size. They are being fed monkey chow. These bears aren't monkeys, so they shouldn't be fed monkey food."

The timing was perfect. The maintenance guy came walking in our direction with a pail of food and the photographer followed closely as I approached him.

"Hi," I said. "I brought some fruit and crayfish to feed the bears. They need more than just monkey chow."

He was surprised by the ambush. "Sorry, kid. I just do what I'm told. I'd get in trouble if I did anything else."

The reporter cut in, "What do you think about these bears' conditions? This young man is concerned about their well-being."

"Ah. They have been here forever," he said. "They get to lie around and have food brought to them. It seems like a good life to me."

I imagined stuffing two handfuls of monkey chow into his mouth and locking him in his tiny maintenance shed. It would have been a little less breezy than the bears' cage, but comparably terrible conditions for a man his size. I remembered Sybil had asked me to observe my rage and practice diplomacy, which helped me come back to reality. This guy was just doing his job.

The reporter told my mom and me that this would be tomorrow's front-page story. Those three words—Front. Page. Story—sounded like sweet revenge on the mayor for hanging up on me. I could hardly contain myself.

I was even more delighted the next morning when the woman who sent me the letter about the bears called our house, shocked to see me on the front page of the paper. She read me the article:

A fourteen-year-old animal activist has been hounding Roseville officials to put a little fun and more nutritious meals into the Royer Park bears' lives. Justin Barker, president of Citizens Lobbying for Animals in Zoos, says the zoo needs some serious improvements after getting a letter from a local resident.

Mayor Vern Fernsby says he is open to arranging a meeting with Justin in order to hear what he has to say. "We all want what is best for the bears and the city is trying to be responsive to Justin's requests."

"Wow. That's unbelievable!" I said, interrupting her. A few nights ago, the mayor hung up on me. Is that what he calls responsive?

"That's called politics and what happens when you get a call from a news reporter," she said. She was impressed, and I was inspired by the coverage.

I wanted to take full advantage of the situation and figured breakfast was the perfect time to call the mayor. I dialed his home number and he answered right away. He didn't sound pleased when he realized it was me. He told me that it wasn't that much of an achievement to get on the front page of a small-town paper, but after he agreed to arrange a meeting with me, I knew he was wrong. It had been less than three days from his hang up and his tone had completely changed. I went from being a whining voice over the phone to a front-page nuisance he couldn't ignore.

My mom was really entertained by the spectacle, listening to the call as she cooked me breakfast, and she agreed to take me to meet the mayor the next day.

He met us at four p.m. on the dot and was accompanied by two men. They were all short, balding, white men with rosy cheeks. They could have been triplets. We shook hands. The mayor explained that these guys were head of Parks and Rec and were in charge of the bears. He added that I should direct all further calls to them and one of them handed me his business card. His name was Ron. I asked if the number on the card was his home phone number and when he said no, I asked for it. The mayor looked at him and widened his eyes. Ron wasn't sure what to say.

"This number is fine," I said, trying to end the awkward moment. I grabbed the long reporter's pad from my back pocket and got right into it, reading my list of demands for the bears:

Change their food to omnivore chow and make sure they get fresh fruit every day and fish three times a week.

Build an addition to the cage that has a gate that can close so the keepers can clean the main cage properly.

Once that addition is built, move the bears in there and add dirt to the main cage so they don't have to constantly walk on concrete.

The man who gave me his card spoke up. "We can probably change their diet, but there is no money to build a larger cage for these bears. We have a long list of priorities."

"Well, would you be willing to move them somewhere else if you can't improve their conditions here?" I asked.

All the men just shook their heads no. The mayor chimed in with an indignant voice. "These bears have been here all their lives. They were born in this town and they will die here."

Something happened in that moment. His tone. The certainty of his voice. His dismissiveness. The idea that the bears would die in this horrible place triggered something in me. It wasn't frustration or anger. It was complete clarity. Everything flashed before my eyes. I knew my mission: I was going to prove Vern Fernsby and the red cheeks wrong and free Brutus and Ursula.

"So, if I can find a home for the bears, you would be open to moving them?" I asked, ignoring the mayor's obscene comment.

They all looked at each other and chuckled at my insistence.

"No one wants to take these bears. We've tried," Ron said. "We can start feeding them some fruit. Would that make you happy?"

"Yes. That's great," I said. I acted satisfied, knowing a change in diet was an important first step. "And you'll start feeding them omnivore chow?" I added.

"Yes. We can start ordering a different food," he confirmed.

They just wanted me off their back and they thought some fresh fruit and omnivore chow would do it. We all shook hands and went our different ways.

After talking to the mayor and the men from Parks and Rec, I realized that I needed to get the bears out of that place. There was no money to improve their cage and these men had Brutus and Ursula at the very bottom of their list of priorities, if they were on their list at all. My mom and I talked about the exchange all the way home and by the time we pulled up to the driveway, I had a plan.

"I need the city to agree to release the bears. If they do that, I can find them a new home."

"How will you find them a new home?"

"I can figure that out later. I just need them to agree to release the bears first."

"The mayor was pretty insistent."

"I think he might change his mind if a TV crew shows up. Think about how he responded to that article."

I would have called Noel, my reporter friend at KOVR 13, but she had gotten a new job in San Francisco. I remembered her telling me once about the audience size of each of the TV stations in Sacramento and I decided to call the big one, KCRA 3. The news desk transferred me to a producer who was a vegetarian. She loved the story.

The following week, as I raced home from school and turned the corner, I saw a news truck sitting in our driveway. I pulled up next to it, waving at a big guy with a handlebar mustache in the driver's seat, and was shocked to see Edie Lambert, one of the main anchors, sitting in the passenger seat. The back door of the van opened and a woman with long flowing hair and jeans stepped out. She looked like a typical vegetarian who shopped at the natural food co-op.

They set up the lights and cameras in our living room and Edie interviewed me for what felt like forever. All I could think about were my braces and how hot it was in the room under all those lights.

I was getting ready for school the next morning when my mom screamed my name from downstairs.

"Get in here! You're on television."

I went running in and caught the last few seconds of what looked like a commercial.

"A boy and his bears. Tonight at five p.m. From Northern California's number one news team, KCRA 3."

My mom was shocked. "They didn't tell us you were going to be on tonight. You looked good—and sounded so articulate!"

She told me she would drive me to school so I could see the teaser during the next commercial break, but the promo never showed. I stepped into homeroom right as the bell rang. One of the girls who lived behind our house waved me over. She was wearing a Selena shirt, and had three-inch curled bangs. "I saw you on TV this morning," she said.

"Yeah, I saw you, too," one of the class clowns chimed in. "Bear Boy is on the news tonight," he said, announcing it to the class like a carnival barker.

I spent most of my time at school trying to be invisible, so I wasn't sure what to think about the attention I was getting. I braced for the normal taunts, but they didn't come. Kids were genuinely admiring me, at least for that moment; it didn't mean I had anyone to talk to or eat lunch with, but I was just happy that no one was being mean. I sped home that afternoon and my mom greeted me at the door.

"Sweetie. You won't believe how many calls I got today. They have been playing the commercial all day. Your aunts saw you, people at work were calling, the neighbors came over."

"Yeah. Kids at school saw it, too," I said.

"This is so great!" My mom seemed really proud, something I hadn't felt from her in a long time.

My dad got home just as the newscast began.

"Tonight, doctors warn that your favorite diet pills might be deadly. Good evening, I'm Lois Hart and I'm Dave Walker. Also tonight, Tom will have your extended seven-day forecast and you'll meet a young man on a mission to help two friends living in un-BEAR-able conditions."

After warnings about diet drugs, a story of a three-alarm fire, and a hit-and-run, it happened: Brutus and Ursula and my crooked teeth appeared on the screen. I was a little embarrassed but happy people were getting to know the bears.

"They haven't done anything wrong, but they have been sentenced to a life in prison," I said.

"We are doing everything we can to work with Justin to help these bears," the mayor retorted.

There he was again. Saying one thing to me and another thing to the media. That was another thing I learned about adults: they weren't so different than kids in their willingness to lie to get what they want.

My mom clapped with excitement and my dad lowered the volume of the TV. "How cool is that?" he said.

And it *was* cool. The phone rang all evening from family, my animal rights friends, and people my parents knew. They all asked what they could do to help me help the bears, so I gave every one of them the mayor's home number. I saved my call to him till the following morning.

6

My calls to the mayor had never felt all that helpful, but I had kept calling anyway. Something about speaking up for Brutus and Ursula and calling the mayor at home was kinda fun for me. I wanted the mayor to know that I was not going anywhere, *and* I would not rest until Brutus and Ursula were on his list of priorities. I called so often I memorized his number.

As I pressed each digit early that morning after the TV spot, I wondered how many people had called his house the night before to complain about the bears. I imagined he was inundated with so many calls that I would get a busy signal, or maybe a message that he had changed his number completely.

But just like the last few times I had called, his message machine picked up.

I was in the middle of leaving a long message when the mayor picked up. He had a totally different tone in his voice.

"Justin. What can I do for you?" he asked, words he had never said before.

I realized the TV show, much like the newspaper article, must have had an impact on him and I decided to call him out on his blatant lies. "Hey, Vern. You said on the news last night that you're doing everything you can to work with me, but that's not exactly true." I paused to let him answer. I really wanted to know why he thought he could say one thing on TV but do another in real life. I'd be grounded for lying to my parents. I certainly wasn't going to let him get away with it.

"Well, we've changed the bears' diet. I've been taking all your calls. What else do you want?"

"I want you to agree to release the bears, so I can find a new home for them."

"You heard what Ron said. No one wants two old bears."

"If I can find them a new home, would you release them?"

"Kid, you are really insistent." He chuckled. "Fine. If you can find a better home for those two, I'll recommend that we let the bears go there."

I couldn't believe it. I thanked the mayor and jumped off the call.

Where could I find a better home? I opened the directory of US Zoos I had gotten during my work at the Sacramento Zoo. There were three hundred and fifty zoos listed. I was slightly overwhelmed by the idea of calling all of those zoos and I felt conflicted about sending Brutus and Ursula to another place where they would spend their lives on display. One of my animal rights friends helped me realize that anywhere was better than where the bears were living now, so I knew the zoos were the right place to start. I was also worried about what my parents would do about all those long-distance calls. With every call I made to each zoo, I was one step closer to another screaming match. I decided Brutus and Ursula were worth the risk.

I closed my eyes, randomly flipped through the book, and landed my finger on the page to the Denver Zoo. I rang the number and was transferred to the director. He told me that bears don't attract crowds and that even

Klondike and Snow, their two famous polar bear cubs, had lost the public's interest since they had grown big.

I spent a week calling one zoo after the other, dialing the East Coast before school and the West Coast when I got home. As I worked my way through the directory, from the Bronx to San Diego to Detroit to St. Louis, there was not a single hint of interest from any of them. It became pretty clear that there was a list of animals that drove zoo attendance and two aging black bears were not on that list. I felt sickened by each director's response and I was sad no one had any interest in Brutus and Ursula's story. Maybe Ron from Parks and Rec was right: people really didn't want black bears.

I was pretty bummed out by the long line of rejections I had gotten all week. Even the warm spring weather on the way to school couldn't help my mood. I spent the first two periods worried that Vern Fernsby was right when he told me Brutus and Ursula would die in Roseville. Things didn't get any better during third period when I faced the two most dreaded letters in middle school: PE. It was always the worst part of my day. I was forced into the locker room with a bunch of boys, made to strip and change in front of our teachers, who sat at their desks staring at us through big windows that covered one whole wall of the locker room. When things got rowdy, they would tap on the thick glass—just like poorly behaved children at the zoo. And things always got rowdy.

When I started seventh grade, I had begged my parents to buy me a forty-eight-pack of white T-shirts at Costco. I was so happy they agreed because I couldn't imagine revealing my awkward body and the hair that started growing on my chest that year. I wore the shirts under my other shirts, so I never had to get fully naked in front of the other kids, but that didn't always stop the insults. People called me fat and made fun of how I swung a bat and how slow I ran. PE was always the worst.

I hurried in from track after a timed mile that day and was changing as fast as I could when I glanced over just as Daniel dropped his underwear. The second his eyes caught mine I knew I was done for.

"Why are you staring at me, fag?" he asked, loud enough so the entire class could hear.

"There's a faggot in the locker room, everyone, hide your junk," one of his friends yelled, his words echoing for all to hear. The whole room erupted in a mix of laughter and panic. My face instantly heated up. I pulled my jeans on, buckled my belt, and grabbed my backpack. As

I hurried past the showers, two jocks covered themselves, looked at each other, and laughed. The second I got into the hall, I burst into tears. I didn't understand why kids were so horrible and why they had to choose that week of all weeks to target me.

I wanted to jump on my bike and race home to call Sybil but jetted towards the library instead. The librarian was my best bet. She knew how mean the kids could be and I knew she would listen to me. I wiped the tears off my face as I walked through the doors, but that didn't stop the librarian from noticing something was wrong. I told her about what had happened in the locker room and what a terrible week it was, making calls about the bears and getting all those no's. She apologized for the boys and promised me that things would get better in high school. I appreciated her kindness and I wanted to believe her, but all I could think about were the jeers and the laughter bouncing off the cinder block walls. Regular counseling sessions with my parents were helping things at home, but there was nothing Sybil or my parents could do to stop the cruelty I endured at school.

When I finally got home that day, I felt paralyzed and sad. I couldn't imagine calling another zoo or hearing another no. I just wanted to turn on Nickelodeon and not think about the day or the week. It had been a long time since I had just relaxed on the couch, and zoning out in front of the tube seemed like a great idea. I flipped to Nickelodeon just in time to catch my favorite part of the game show *Family Double Dare*: the obstacle course. A family would run through various messy challenges to win prizes. A redheaded girl had just jumped on top of two six-foot-wide waffles covered in a bathtub's worth of maple syrup and topped with a massive scoop of fake butter.

Her whole body was dripping in syrup, her face covered with the buttery substance. She handed a flag to her dad, who jumped through a foam wringer and into a pool of slime. He grabbed the orange flag just as the buzzer went off, winning $7,000 in prizes and a family trip to Paris. What used to be so entertaining to me just a year ago, now felt shallow and useless. The green slime the entire family was covered in as they jumped up and down celebrating their win made me think about the algae that Ursula spent her days slipping on as she paced around her cage. *What am I doing?* I clicked off the TV and went to the kitchen to call Doris.

Sybil helped me work through my personal challenges, and Doris helped me navigate the struggles I faced as an activist. I told her how many zoos I had called over the last week and the equal number of no's I had heard. When I first told her about my plan, she was pretty skeptical about the idea of the bears moving to another zoo. Instead of the *"I told you so"* I was expecting from her, she pleaded for me to have patience and explained that if I was going to sustain my activism, I was going to have to get comfortable with lots of rejection and failure. Doris was an old-school activist and she had seen it all. She always had stories to tell and that day, she told me about an eighty-year-old French activist.

"Every day for twenty years she has stood at the same intersection holding the same sign that says, *Go Vegetarian.* Despite the daily challenges she faces, she's committed. Not her frail body, the rain, or the beating sun can stop her. She faces jeers and laughter from the passers-by in a land of foie gras and horse steaks. She may never know if her actions inspire anyone to change their diet, but she stands there anyway. That's what good activists do."

"They do what?" I asked, unsure of how her story related to my own horrible week.

"You can't let a little rain or a bunch of bozos stop you from continuing down the path."

"Then what should I do?"

"Forget about the zoos. You should call the Performing Animal Welfare Society. Pat might have some advice for you. She might even be able to take the bears."

PAWS had helped me understand the bears' dietary needs, but it didn't even dawn on me they might be able to take them. I was so excited at this idea. I thanked Doris and called immediately. Pat Derby was a former Hollywood animal trainer who had started a thirty-acre sanctuary about five miles from my house. The more I thought about it, the more I thought it would be the perfect place for Ursula and Brutus. They could retire with the elephants, tigers, baboons, and hundreds of other former animal entertainers from films, circuses, and zoos.

I was convinced that a single call to PAWS would do the trick. I just knew that Pat would love the bears' story and could find room for Brutus and Ursula.

I was wrong. I left a message, and when Pat eventually called me back, she explained that the four bears they already had were more bears than they could handle and that she couldn't take Brutus and Ursula. My heart sank. Zoos didn't want them, sanctuaries didn't either. I just wanted to hang up, but instead, I asked if she had any ideas about who might be able to take the bears.

"Call Terry at Folsom Zoo, they are a rescue zoo who might be able to help. I feel like I heard something about their bears recently," Pat said.

I would have normally hung up the phone and dialed the number immediately, but I couldn't take another no. I retreated to my room and plopped on my bed. I just lay there, thinking about how trapped I felt and how horrible the bears must feel in their cage in Roseville. I imagined them running through the woods, sleeping on piles of redwood needles, fishing in the river for food.

My dad yelled my name from the kitchen. I sprang up from my daydream and braced myself for impact. The phone bill must have arrived. I tried ignoring his yells, but by the fourth and loudest I didn't have a choice. I jumped up and opened my door.

"Did you call my name, Pops?"

"You need to take out the trash."

I hated taking out the trash, but this time I did it without a complaint. I was just relieved Dad wasn't yelling to discuss *another three hundred and fifty dollars down the drain.* I knew the phone bill would arrive soon and that he would, inevitably, be yelling again.

I had a small window to call Folsom Zoo so I woke up early the next morning, dialed the number Pat had given me, and asked for Terry, the zoo director. I had talked to a lot of directors and she was the first one who actually sounded interested in what I had to say. She knew all about Brutus and Ursula since they were only a few towns over. I told her about what I had done to improve their diet and that I was concerned that they might not survive another flood season. I told her that the mayor had agreed to release the bears and how many zoos I had called looking for a new home for them. Terry's tone made me think that moving the bears to Folsom might be a real possibility, but I still feared she was going to say the exact same thing the other directors had said.

"You know, Justin," she said. "I got a similar call a few years ago from a woman in Roseville and I had to tell her that we couldn't help the bears…"

I braced myself as I waited for her no.

"We were right in the middle of building the new mountain lion enclosure when she called, so we couldn't even think about taking the bears. But we've just finished that project and, interestingly, you've called at the perfect time because building a new bear complex is our next focus.

I jumped up. "Really?"

"We have two bears named Ensign and Fisher. The first phase of our bear enclosure is meant for them. The second phase will have room for four additional bears. I can't guarantee anything but there is a chance that we might be able to move the plans around and get Brutus and Ursula here as part of that first phase and then move Ensign and Fisher later on."

I didn't know what yes would sound like or where it would come from, but this seemed like yes. "Wow," I said. "That would be amazing!"

"I don't want to get your hopes up quite yet," Terry said. "Let me talk with some people here and get back to you."

My hopes were more than up! I just knew that Terry would call me back to tell me she could take the bears.

Indeed, a day or so later, Terry called back. She told me that she had spoken with the keeper team and the director of the nonprofit that fundraised for the zoo.

"What did they say?" I asked, eager to get the news. Terry could hear the excitement in my voice and laughed a little bit.

"Well. I have good news and I have bad news," she said. She was really drawing this thing out. "The good news is that we can take Brutus and Ursula."

"Oh my God! Really?" I leapt out of my chair and began jumping up and down. I couldn't contain myself. "That is amazing! That's the best news I have ever gotten! Thank you so much!" I paused in the midst of the excitement and realized that I hadn't heard the whole story. "What's the bad news?" I asked.

"The bad news is that it will take a minimum of $250,000 to build them a new home. It took us almost five years to raise that much money to get the mountain lion exhibit built."

"Woah. That's a lot of money," I said.

"That is the thing. It *is* a lot of money and we can only agree to take the bears if someone comes up with it."

I had gotten pies donated for Thanksgivings when we fed the homebound elderly and sold cookies to raise money for our school each year, but a quarter of a million dollars sounded like an impossible amount of money to raise. I had no idea where the money would come from, but I didn't hesitate in vowing to raise it.

"I will raise the money," I said. "I'll do whatever I need to do to get Brutus and Ursula out of there.

7

I plopped on my pillow and thought about how
the worst few weeks of my life had just turned into
the best. Someone could take the bears, Roseville had
agreed to release them, and all I needed to do was come
up with a quarter of a million dollars to build them a
new home. I was thrilled at the prospect of getting Brutus and Ursula out of Roseville, but the idea of raising
that much money was completely overwhelming to me.
I thought about the eighty-year-old French woman with
her sign at that busy Parisian intersection and about the
tortoise from Aesop's fable. *Slow and steady wins the race,
slow and steady wins the race,* I repeated in my head. But
then I thought, *Slow and steady means that the bears could
face another flood season—or five flood seasons if I don't*

move fast enough. The first thing I did was what I was best at. I flipped through my Rolodex and dialed every person I thought should hear the news, totally ignoring that it was eight in the morning.

I called Mom and Dad last. They had both just gotten to work. They were happy for me but more concerned that I hadn't left for school yet. I rolled my eyes; summer was on its way and soon they couldn't pester me about school. I'd no longer have to spend my mornings racing to beat that first-period bell or all day dodging petty assholes. I sped to school and endured the morning. I told the librarian the news about the bears at lunch and after school raced home to tell Doris. She thought the news was so cool and wanted to know my plan. I told her a bunch of ideas about how I would raise that much money and also admitted about being a little scared about if I could do it.

"Creating change is just like walking," she said. "If you know your destination, all you have to do is put one foot in front of the other and keep moving and you'll get there."

I thought about that for a minute and decided that one step at a time *was* possible. She then asked me what my next step would be.

"If I am going to ask people to donate, I need a place where people can send money."

I got off the phone with Doris to call a few banks, figuring it would be easy to set up a bank account. After five or so calls to the big banks, I realized the auto attendant and call center operators could care less about my story or the bears' plight. A week later I was in the car running errands with my mom telling her about my struggle when a radio commercial came on.

"When you call Bank of the West we will answer."

I looked at my mom and it was as if they were talking directly to me. The perfectly timed commercial surprised us both.

"I guess I have to call Bank of the West," I said

"They will answer," my mom said, mocking the ad.

We laughed.

I got home, flipped through the phone book, dialed the bank, and sure enough, someone answered on the third ring.

"Bank of the West, this is Mary."

I told Mary all about the bears and she actually *listened* to me. Even better, she loved the story about my fight to free the bears and their perfectly timed commercial. I asked if it was at all possible to set up a bank account for the bears. She put me on hold for what felt like forever. A man picked up the phone and it was the branch manager. He told me his name was Alan and he was pretty sure he could help if we could stop by the bank. My mom agreed to take me after school the next day. When we pulled into the parking lot, my mouth dropped at the sight of the bank's logo: it was a bear.

We walked into the lobby and there were bears all over the place. A large poster with a mama bear and her cubs promoting low percentage housing loans, a cardboard cutout of a grizzly, and huge pile of stuffed bears with a sign that said, "*Free bear with all new accounts.*" It all felt surreal. The radio commercial coming on when it did. Walking into a bank full of bears. My mom seemed just as moved as I was.

"I think it's meant to be," she whispered to me, reaching down and squeezing my hand.

We walked to the first available teller and it was Mary—another crazy coincidence. She was so happy to see me and she walked around to the front and reached her arms out.

"I just have to give you a big hug. What you're doing for those bears is fantastic." She turned to my mom and gave her a hug as well. "Thank you for raising such an amazing young man. You must be proud."

"We are very proud of him," my mom said. "If he could only get the phone bills under control."

Mary grabbed the stuffed bear that was sitting on her desk and handed it to me. "This one is for you," she said, ushering us over to the manager's office. He was on the phone but flashed a big smile and waved us in.

"I have to go," he told the person on the phone. "A VIP just walked into my office."

He jumped off the phone and welcomed me, telling us about how all the people at HQ and at the branch had heard the story about the bears and how excited they were to support it.

"If you didn't notice, we really like bears here," Alan said, looking around and gesturing to the bear in my lap.

We talked through the plan and he agreed that his team could manage all of the incoming mail and then he asked me what I wanted to call the project. I thought for a moment and then it rolled off my tongue. "Let's call it 'The Roseville Bear Relocation Fund.'"

"So, one last thing," he said as my mom and I cosigned the application. "We need to deposit money into the account to make it official. How much money have you raised so far?"

I looked at my mom and then I looked at him. "Well...I haven't raised any money yet," I said, stumbling over my words. "That's why I'm setting up the account."

"Oh. That's okay. You'll have to deposit at least one hundred dollars to officially open the account. We'll input all your information today. Once you have one hundred dollars, we can open it officially."

The second my mom and I walked out of the doors. I pleaded for her to give me one hundred dollars to open the account, but she shook her head no.

"Sweetie, this is your project. I'm going to let you figure out how to raise the first one hundred dollars. It would be too easy if I just handed it to you."

"Mom. Please. I promise I will pay you back," I begged.

"I'm not going to give you the money. We are already paying part of the phone bills for you. I know that you will figure it out."

"Okay, wait," I said, stopping in the parking lot. I was so frustrated. "I'm going to go back into the bank to see how much they actually love bears."

Mom smiled and shook her head. "Okay. I'll be in the car."

I walked back into the bank. Alan was talking with Mary at her desk and I walked right up to them. "I think it would be really cool if Bank of the West could make the first donation to the bear fund." I held up the stuffed bear, squeezed it, and raised my eyebrows.

Alan got a big grin on his face, gestured for me to wait with Mary, and went to his office. He came back with a concerned look on his face. "I spoke with my district manager. I'm sorry, but we can't donate one hundred dollars to the fund."

"Okay," I said, feeling disappointment rise up in me.

He smiled. "We are going to donate five hundred dollars to the fund."

Mary shrieked at the news and smacked Alan on the arm. "You joker. That's fantastic!"

I couldn't believe it. "Thank you so much! That is so cool!"

He tossed me another stuffed bear. "There are two bears, right?"

"Yes! Brutus and Ursula."

If I judged humanity based on Nancy and the kids at my junior high school, the future looked pretty bleak. But just an hour at Bank of the West, meeting Mary and Alan, gave me a whole new perspective on things. I was amazed that two perfect strangers could treat me with such kindness and extend such generosity. I went running to the car to give my mom the news and thanked her for not giving me the cash I begged for. In that moment, I saw her differently, too. I realized she was doing her job—helping me understand the world, empowering me to ask for the things I needed, and encouraging me to stand up for the things I felt passionate about. I had actually never felt this passionate about anything in my life. Not my work at the Sacramento Zoo, not my vegetarianism, not our annual Thanksgiving feedings of the homebound.

Saving Brutus and Ursula became my full-time obsession and the bank account meant people could officially write checks. It was on! I rushed home from the bank to call an animal rescue organization whose program manager had promised to donate once they could write a check and I was surprised by how much the board of directors had agreed to give—one thousand dollars.

"You couldn't have timed this better," I explained, after thanking him over and over. I was meeting a reporter from a neighborhood newspaper the following day and was excited to tell him we had raised fifteen hundred dollars in less than twenty-four hours. I was reading him the bank address to send the check when my dad screamed my name from the kitchen and tugged on the phone cord. I finished the call as quickly as I could and came into the kitchen where I saw the phone bill opened on the table. My heart sank.

Before he could speak, I tried to change the subject. "Did Mom tell you what happened today? Bank of the West donated five hundred dollars and I just got off the phone with an organization who just donated one thousand dollars."

"Of course you just got off the phone," he said, holding up the bill and fanning through the pages. It was as thick as a *National Geographic.*

"Justin, you keep promising to talk less on the phone, but the bills keep getting bigger and bigger," my dad said, shaking his head in disappointment. "Do you see how many pages this is?"

Luckily, summer was only a few weeks away and I'd return to the land of free phone calls at the Animal Protection Institute. It meant I could actually follow through on my promise to my parents to use the phone less and that I would have the chance to spend every waking hour focused on the bears.

I learned quickly that the more media attention the bears got, the quicker the relocation fund grew. I got to know the assignment editors at each of the local TV stations and befriended reporters at the regional newspapers. Whether it was an update about how much money the fund had raised or an appearance I was making at an elementary school, I somehow always found a spotlight for the bears and myself. Wherever we landed, I always asked them to include the address where people could send checks—and it worked.

Every appearance averaged two hundred and fifty dollars in donations and inspired a flood of mail. Every week the bank would process the avalanche of letters and would send me a large envelope with the correspondence and a receipt updating me on how much money we had raised. There were envelopes with five-dollar checks, some with hundreds, and others with thousands. There were long gushing letters from people who knew the bears well and short notes from people who were surprised by my age. Some apologized for not sending enough and others promised they would donate monthly. There were office secretaries who put donation jars on counters, tennis coaches who ran fundraising matches, old ladies who shared their social security, and kids who donated their allowance. There were perfectly scribed notes, long typed letters, craft paper with doodles, and sloppily penned cards. Some insisted I send regular updates and others requested no acknowledgment. There were Smiths, Wongs, McMillans, and Kapoors. I got blessed, prayed for, and had good energy sent my way. There were fellow animal activists, and others who were inspired that one person could create change in the world. Sometimes I would get little notes from the bank tellers telling me that opening those letters was their favorite part of their workday. I loved seeing how much people cared and how the story of Brutus and Ursula could inspire such generosity.

While the five-dollar checks were really sweet, I realized it would take 50,000 of them to move the bears. Winter and the threat of floods were only six months away. Brutus and Ursula lived on the edge of a creek on a floodplain and I was worried that they would be darted, relocated, and traumatized by an emergency move if a big storm hit, or worse, swept them away to their deaths. I decided I couldn't rely on the generosity of the Valley alone and decided to take the bears' plight to a national audience.

Luckily, I found a large stack of media directories at API. There was a directory for TV, newspapers, and radio. Each was thick as a phone book with the names and phone numbers of hundreds if not thousands of TV producers, news desk editors, and reporters from all over the country. I called NBC, ABC, and CBS, both their news divisions and morning shows. I called producers at *Oprah, Maury Povich, Sally Jessy Raphael*, and *Montel Williams*—all popular talk shows at the time. I called shows I had watched and shows I had never heard of. There was one thing in common as I worked my way through the endless list—TV people were not that friendly and always sounded like they had something better to do. I'd get a lot of rejections, hang-ups, and transfers to voicemail, but I didn't let it get me down. I figured with three large directories there was someone who would want to do a story about the bears and all I needed to do was just keep calling. There were no's from the *Today* show, *Inside Edition*, *Hard Copy*, and *The Jim J. and Tammy Faye Show*. I thought it would be so cool to be on Nickelodeon, but even *Nick News with Linda Ellerbee* said no. If I had made a dollar for every no I got in those weeks of outreach, I would have raised a lot of money for the bears.

But one afternoon I found the phone number and the name for a producer of one of my favorite shows, *The Crusaders*. It was a syndicated show about a group of reporters who went beyond the usual news stories to find injustices in the world and then fought to make them right. I had seen an episode where one of the crusaders had gotten wolf hunting banned in Alaska and I thought this could be my chance.

I dialed the number and the woman who answered sounded more friendly than anyone else I had talked to. She loved my story about the bears and told me that it would have made the perfect segment, if their show had not been cancelled. It was so sad to hear that such a good show would soon be pulled off the air—and it taught me that even adults with really good ideas can get rejected, too.

"Yeah, we are all pretty bummed about it. We all put our heart and soul into it," she said. "How about this? One of our reporters, Carla, just started a new gig on an NBC show called *Real Life*. She's an animal person. Let me pitch this idea to her and see what she thinks."

Thirty minutes later the phone rang. It was Carla. She not only loved the story but her executive producer had greenlit the production.

"It means that I'm going to come to your town with a camera crew and do a story about the bears," she explained, telling me that the show aired across the country and averaged two million viewers a day.

Within a few weeks Carla arrived with a cameraman and audio tech. I spent two days introducing them to the bears, having them interview my parents, and filming the hillside where the bears would hopefully one day reside at the Folsom Zoo. A week later my mom and I sat on the couch with breakfast and I hit record on our VCR. We watched, anxiously waiting, and then after what felt like the tenth commercial break, the anchor said my name.

"Time now for you to meet a very special person. His name is Justin Barker."

My mom and I both screamed in excitement.

When he was in second grade he went on a trip to the zoo, sure, like many of us, he would love to see the animals and learn about them. But instead of being awed by the animals, Justin was appalled at the conditions they were forced to live in—in fact, the sight of a tiger living in a cramped cage brought him to tears.

I looked at my mom. "It wasn't a tiger. It was a black-footed cat."

"Close enough," she said quietly, patting my leg for us to listen.

"Justin Barker isn't your average fourteen-year-old," Carla said over a video montage of kids from my neighborhood. "You won't find him hanging out with the guys, he doesn't have time to skateboard or fish or ride bikes, and the only girl he has eyes for is Ursula."

My cheeks heated up instantly. Carla's words repeated in my head over and over. *The only girl he has eyes for is Ursula.* Not only had she just told the world I was a loner, but she had also hinted at a secret I thought that I had successfully hidden.

Ursula was the only *girl* I had eyes for, and every time the bullies at school called me a fag—a word whose meaning I finally learned—they were onto something. I had spent the last three years grappling with my attraction to guys, turning to AOL chat rooms to ask strangers all the questions that swirled in my head—What did "gay" mean? When would you "officially" know? What was sex like?

At first, I thought I'd get over the feelings once puberty passed. I even wondered if my fantasies about men were more about admiration than attraction. Maybe I was so desperate to grow up that I envied grown men? I wasn't sure about any of it, but I was totally humiliated that two million people might understand Carla's words the way I did.

I almost missed the entire segment but came to just in time to hear the anchors invite people to donate to the project by calling their information line.

"That was really good, honey," my mom said, totally missing the fact that I had just spent the last five minutes in my head, not at all seeing the same show she had.

"Let's watch it again," I said, crawling across the carpet toward the TV and rewinding the VCR. I was actually really happy once I was able to see the entire segment and I hoped the exposure the bears got would make up for my humiliation.

A few hours later, my mom dropped me off at API, where the receptionist greeted me with a note about a missed call. It was from Carla and it was marked urgent.

I called her back right away and she sounded ecstatic.

"Justin. Our phone lines have been ringing all morning. Our operators can't keep up with the number of people who want to help the bears. We have never seen anything like this."

People's interest in the bears started pouring in—along with their donations. Those five minutes of airtime inspired a slew of checks, letters, and phone calls from all over the country. The messages arrived in droves from New York, Minnesota, Texas, Colorado, and a long list of other places. We raised four thousand dollars from the show. Suddenly, magazines, both big and small, wanted interviews. I got invited to speak at service clubs, and other clubs offered their help and support. A kind man from the foothills outside of Sacramento offered to build a website for the bears and a woman in Alaska donated a percentage of all the money her bed and breakfast earned each month.

I learned I wasn't the only one who was fielding calls and receiving letters about the bears. Vern Fernsby's office was receiving a barrage of complaints about the conditions the bears faced. The flood of complaints after the national story ran helped me as I increased the pressure on the city to do more for Brutus and Ursula. I was so relentless in my requests that they financially contributed to the relocation fund and improved the bears' conditions while they waited for their new home. For so long the Roseville civic leaders had refused to contribute any money and were incredulous at the idea of doing anything to improve the bears' cage.

"Why would we invest in a cage that is going to be torn down?" Ron, the head of Parks and Rec, and the mayor would ask when I made my regular calls to them.

I would say the same thing every time: "This is not about the cage. This is about two living, breathing animals for whom you are responsible."

The media spotlight must have begun to wear Vern Fernsby down because a few weeks after the NBC show aired, I got a call from the Folsom Zoo director, who told me she had just gotten off the phone with the city. I couldn't believe my ears. The mayor had promised $50,000 toward the project, meaning close to $70,000 had been raised. I would have never guessed that Vern Fernsby would actually step up. It was a huge win.

There was one success after the other that summer, both at home and for the bears. Being able to focus on something I loved and to make all the calls I wanted from API had really improved the dynamics between me and my parents. We were fighting less and were learning to enjoy each other's company again. Ninth grade was starting in just a few weeks, and I was looking forward to a fresh start at a whole new campus.

During those last weeks of summer, my parents and I decided to spend an afternoon together at the Folsom Zoo. It was the first time we had visited all together. The zoo director took us to the undeveloped hillside that Brutus and Ursula would one day call home. We struggled to keep up through the tall grasses but enjoyed the shade of the towering oak trees. Our socks were covered in prickers when we returned to the path and we sat on a bench across from a young mountain lion laughing as we pulled them off our cuffs. The zoo director returned with a large roll of paper and, on the picnic table nearby, unrolled the architect's plans for the bears' habitat.

"It will be ten times the size of their current home," she said, pointing to the hillside where we had just walked and describing how it would be transformed. "We are keeping all the trees. We'll build a waterfall and heated pool, a sandy area where they can dig, and two large rock dens so they can retreat from public view and the elements."

We were all moved by the plans for the bears and talked about how amazing it all was as we walked back to the car.

My dad squeezed my shoulder. "I am really proud of what you are doing for Brutus and Ursula."

My mom agreed. "You've really amazed us this summer."

It really seemed like everything would work out.

Just three days later, my parents dropped a bomb that threatened to ruin all my hard work, my new-found confidence, and the bears' future.

8

Just seventy-two hours before I was starting ninth grade, Mom and Dad sat me down at the dinner table and broke the terrible news.

"We're moving to Costa Rica," Dad said.

"We're going to spend six months learning Spanish there," Mom explained.

"You'll start school on Monday and do your first semester here, then we'll move just after Christmas," Dad continued.

The look on their faces made it seem as if they thought I would be excited by the news. I was totally shocked. My family had taken a cruise to Mexico when I was eight. I loved experiencing the food and culture there, but that was for a week, not six months, and not now. Why would they pull me away from the bears at this pivotal moment? How would I ever make friends if I spent half of the first year of high school in a foreign country? Who would make sure the bears were cared for while I was gone? I had so many questions and just as much anger about the news.

"We can learn Spanish here!" I said.

"You go, and I'll stay," I said.

"What if we just go next summer?" I said.

I pleaded, begged, and suggested for them to rethink the move without success. My dad had already confirmed his sabbatical from work, my mom would take a leave of absence, and I would go to an international school that they had already applied to.

My parents had spent the summer hiding their master plan from me. I had been keeping secrets, too—but I had a really good reason for not sharing mine. I wasn't even really sure how I felt about it and my feelings were changing almost daily. Some days, when I was in the chat rooms and heard stories of being kicked out of the house after coming out, I would be terrified about my attraction to men. On other days, when I allowed myself to think about going to a dance or going out on a date, I would get lost in happy fantasies.

But none of the feelings that *I* was keeping secret in my head had anything to do with my parents. The secret *they* had been keeping would impact my life in a massive way. I was furious at them both.

"Why would you do this without asking me what I thought first?" I asked.

"We decided to go, so you're going, too," Mom said.

"What about Shane?" I asked, mentioning my older brother who lived in an apartment in town; he had been doing his own thing since he moved out and we only saw him once a month or so. "Are you making him go, too?"

"He's twenty. You're fourteen. You still have to do what we say."

I insisted we go to Sybil to negotiate the plans; she always helped me defend myself against what I saw as their irrational behavior. I thought for sure she would agree with me that this harebrained idea needed rethinking. I was wrong. As I talked with Sybil, Doris, and the other adults I trusted in my life, everyone told me the same thing. They said that six months was nothing, that this was an opportunity of a lifetime, and that I should take advantage of it.

Any excitement I had about starting ninth grade was gone as I thought about leaving in the middle of the year.

But that first week back at school surprised me. The librarian was right: things got better in high school. A bunch of kids in my homeroom class had seen the story about the bears and thought it was really cool that I was on TV. At lunch, a few other kids mentioned my TV appearance and I noticed that Daniel and his jerk friends were nowhere to be seen. I talked the lunch lady into getting veggie burgers on the lunch line and I was only a five-minute bike ride from home, giving me an extra twenty minutes every day to double down on my work for the bears. With only four months to go before I would be too far away to do anything, I decided to ditch my plans of making new friends, kept a low profile at school, and spend all my free time focused on Brutus and Ursula.

I had been in plenty of regional newspapers, but I somehow never managed to convince the *Sacramento Bee* that the relocation project was anything more than a pipe dream. The *Bee* landed outside the front door of almost every house and apartment in the Valley's 12,000-square-mile radius. I figured even a mention of the bears somewhere in those pages could be a critical boost to the project. I had spent six months calling the same reporter whenever something happened. I probably talked with her ten times and left just as many messages with updates about the bears. I called when the bank account was opened, I left a message when we reached three thousand dollars in donations, I invited her to watch the NBC show, and I read the most touching letters I'd received to her voicemail. I treated her like a friend who was interested in what was happening with the bears, even though she never asked. Some people would have called my tactics annoying, but I was always polite—and in the end, they worked. One day, I called her with the news that over $70,000 had been raised and mentioned that I would be disappearing to Costa Rica for six months —boom! She was hooked. She arrived at my house two days later, picked me up, and we drove to meet the bears together. She asked me questions about my dreams, my family, and my goals.

I figured she would write a small article that would appear on the back page of the metro section. I woke up the next day, snagged the paper off the porch, and I could not believe my eyes—my face took up most of the *front page* of the metro section.

"Oh my God," I screamed. My parents came downstairs; they were just as surprised as I was.

"You're famous," my dad joked.

My mom made coffee as I read the article out loud:

Justin Barker has just pedaled a half mile home from Laguna Creek High School. His already ruddy cheeks are flushed, and his spectacles have slipped down his nose. Still breathless, he rifles through the day's mail, looking for any correspondence about the two beings that his mother says have given his life purpose. They are Ursula and her brother, Brutus, California black bears caged in a now-defunct zoo in Roseville. For the fourteen-year-old Elk Grove boy, moving the bears into a yet-to-be-built home in Folsom Zoo has become an obsession; protecting the rights of all animals, a lifelong commitment.

Chills went down my spine and tears down my face. I sniffled, struggling to read. I was so touched that she had heard me. Her words reflected what I felt deep inside— that my work was much bigger than Brutus and Ursula, the amount of money that needed to be raised, or the battle that raged between me, Vern Fernsby, and the Roseville Parks and Rec department. This was about justice, standing up for the voiceless, and helping people see that animals were more than food or entertainment. They had their own unique lives and deserved the same decency and respect that we all yearn for. My mom grabbed the paper to help me finish the story. By the end of the article, we were all in tears. The reporter had done such a beautiful job in sharing the bears' story and humanizing mine.

We were not the only people touched by the article. The response was completely overwhelming and almost instantaneous. Our home phone started ringing off the hook from friends, family, and more media. A bunch of radio morning shows wanted interviews, schools invited me to speak to auditoriums full of kids, and local businesses wanted to start fundraising drives. It seemed like half of my homeroom class at school had seen the article and the other half discovered it when our teacher held it up.

"Did anyone see today's paper?" she teased, looking at me.

"Yeah. Bear Boy is on the front cover!" one of the football players yelled out.

My cheeks heated up from the attention and I anticipated ensuing laughter. I was thrown off by what came next: a round of applause and some cheers from my class. I really didn't know how to respond. I had never had this much attention, let alone support from my classmates.

That article attracted all sorts of attention, welcome and unwelcome. I got a letter from an inmate at Folsom

Prison asking me to send photos of myself in a bathing suit and calls from companies who wanted to "align" with the project. Somehow, one corporate radio station convinced me that when I left for Costa Rica, I should hand the fundraising efforts over to them. I was so worried about raising the last $180,000 and so concerned about walking away from Ursula and Brutus, that I said yes.

As our departure for Costa Rica inched closer and closer, there was another article in the newspaper that would impact Brutus and Ursula: "Climate Patterns Hint at Troubling Winter" the headline read. It predicted that our valley might get more rain than the earth could soak up. Roseville was on a floodplain where waters had wiped out whole neighborhoods. The bears were locked in a cage just feet from a creek that had flooded so many times.

During the three weeks before we were booked to fly to the humidity and heat of Costa Rica, I obsessively tracked the news of heavy snows bombarding the mountains just to the east of us. I should have been thrilled to be leaving the suburbs and cold behind, but instead I was a total mess. I was angry at my parents, scared for the bears, and confused about moving so far away. The seven-day countdown to our flight began just as news broke about a string of warm, wet storms that swirled in the Pacific, threatening to take aim at the Valley. The day we took our Christmas tree down and started packing our bags, the rains came and wouldn't let up. It rained and rained, and the snow started to melt. Rivers began to surge, and I watched as violent waters inundated one foothill town after another. The news anchors predicted that the Valley was next, experts described it as unprecedented, and officials declared a state of emergency. We faced an oncoming wall of water.

The day we were scheduled to fly to Costa Rica, I sat on the carpet, just inches from the TV, watching in disbelief as the rivers and creeks overflowed their banks. Families wept as they lost everything, helicopters plucked people from the tops of their cars, and bridges were destroyed, isolating whole towns. Mother Nature was out in full force. Just when Brutus and Ursula needed me most, I would turn my back on them.

"Justin, are you all packed and ready to go?" my mom yelled from the top of the stairs. "I just got a call from Grandma and she says the levees near the airport might give way. We've got to get over there right away." I could hardly look in my mom's direction as tears rolled down my face. I was not getting on that plane with my parents.

"No. I'm not ready, Mom," I yelled. "I'm not going to Costa Rica. You and Dad can go on your highfalutin adventure to learn Spanish alone!"

My mom dragged her large suitcase down the stairs and yelled back, "Justin, you are fourteen years old. Get your suitcase, turn off the TV, and let's go!"

Despite the dreadful tone and volume of my mom's voice, I wasn't going to budge from my spot in front of the TV. I flicked through the commercials trying to find news about Roseville. I was really worried about the bears and I needed to know what was happening.

I flipped to Channel 3 and saw large graphics spin across the screen: *Channel 3 Reports, FloodWatch '97.* "Our team coverage continues where we go to Michael Kidd in Live 'Copter 3, flying over Roseville—one of the many cities hit hard by this New Year's flooding. Michael?"

I turned the volume to max for the whole house to hear. I could feel my heart pounding.

Inside the helicopter's dry interior, the rugged pilot with perfectly slicked hair addressed the camera. "We are high over Roseville where waters continue to rise. Most of the city's residents near these surging creeks were evacuated this morning, but unfortunately, not all of them have been able to escape."

The helicopter's mounted camera zoomed toward the fast-moving waters below—and through the haze and the thick sheets of rain, I saw the outline of the bears' cage.

I screamed and jumped to my feet. Barely visible, I could just make out Brutus and Ursula pacing on the second tier of their cage. "If you can make out what we are looking at here, Brutus and Ursula—those now-famous bears—are trapped in their cage. It is submerged in what looks like three feet of water. I'm really worried about these bears." Michael paused and held his hand to his ear. "I'm hearing that California Fish and Game is working on a rescue plan for these two, but from our vantage point, there is no one in sight."

My stubbornness turned to desperation. "Please don't make me go, please don't make me go," I begged my parents. They forced me to turn off the TV and insisted I get in the car. They both looked scared. We were all scared. I was worried about the bears and my parents were concerned about the impending deluge that threatened to ground our plane.

Rain pelted the windshield as our wipers squeaked back and forth in the minivan. Speeding down a water-logged highway, my mom glared out the window while my dad gripped the steering wheel. Looking in the rearview mirror, he said, "Buddy, I know it must be hard leaving right now. It's really scary out there."

Surrounded by four oversized suitcases, I couldn't control the tears rolling down my face. How could I leave without knowing that Brutus and Ursula would be okay? Looking over her shoulder, my mom reached to touch my leg and softened her tone from earlier. "Honey, I promise things are going to get better once we are all settled in Costa Rica."

"Things aren't going to get better if the bears drown to death in their cage," I sobbed. "I should be there making sure that Brutus and Ursula are okay, not getting on a plane."

"What could you possibly do to help rescue Brutus and Ursula right now?" she asked.

I didn't respond. Other than my sniffles, I was silent for the rest of the way to the airport. I didn't have any more fight in me. I just wanted to know the bears were okay, but I had no way of finding out.

As we walked down the jet bridge toward the airplane, it was as if I could hear every drop of rain pounding overhead. My mom had given me two Benadryl to help me sleep and I was starting to feel groggy.

We took our seats and buckled up. I tried focusing on the long streaming patterns the raindrops made on my window as the plane sped down the runway. I fought my drowsiness, and my worries the bears wouldn't survive, thinking over and over of the words my mother had said: *"What could you possibly do to help rescue Brutus and Ursula right now?"*

I could rescue them, I thought. *I could rescue them....*

─────────

I steered a small motorboat past submerged trees and rooftops toward the bears' cage. Hard rain soaked my thin shirt and filled the bottom of my small boat. As quickly as I wiped the water from my glasses, it collected again. Passing a disappearing playground, the boat slammed into the bears' cage, half consumed by the fast-moving creek.

"Brutus...Ursula," I yelled.

The two bears dog-paddled across the submerged interior of their cage toward me. "I'm gonna get you outta here," I screamed. I gripped the edge of the cage just as Brutus clawed onto the same place. I was surrounded by fast-moving water. I grabbed large wire cutters from the boat and threw them on top of the bear cage. Climbing up the side, I reached the top. I got to work cutting away the thick wire, making quick progress in cutting a bear-sized hole. I pulled the five-by-five-foot section away and screamed for the bears: "Brutus! Ursula!" Both bears paddled towards the submerged platform below the hole. The bears tried climbing toward freedom and I clapped my hands to coax them.

Much larger and stronger than Ursula, Brutus was the first to escape to the top of the cage that was now almost completely filled with water. He shook the water off his fur as Ursula struggled to follow. Both Brutus and I had our eyes locked on Ursula. She clawed the top of the cage as she struggled to pull herself to freedom. She lost her grip, falling back into the water. "Nooooo," I screamed. Brutus huffed and raised his two front paws, slamming the top of the cage, looking for his sister below. Ursula popped her head back up, gasping for air. "Come on. Come on. Come on, girl. You can do it," I yelled. Ursula paddled toward my voice and she struggled to escape. The rising waters helped her gain leverage. She pulled herself free and plopped down from exhaustion.

I turned to get the rope from the motorboat, but it had floated away. Rushing waters raised around us.

Thwop, thwop, thwop...Live 'Copter 3 comes into view as I clear the water from my glasses.

"Ladies and gentlemen, we have started our descent into Juan Santamaria International Airport".

I was startled by the announcement and by my very dry surroundings. No bears. No helicopter. Both my parents were fast asleep. My dad was snoring and my mom was propped up with a neck pillow, her eyes covered. I was partly relieved it was a dream—and instantly panicked about the truth.

9

The sun was just coming up over San Jose when our plane landed in the bustling capital. We grabbed our bags from the luggage claim and filled the back seat of the dingy taxi that would take us to our new home. Our driver tore through morning traffic, erratically slowing and speeding up every few blocks. He turned down narrow streets and up expansive boulevards. We swerved around buses, other taxis, and businessmen who attempted to flag rides. My dad practiced his broken Spanish and my mom and I were huddled together in the back seat, trying to keep the luggage from falling over. I was mesmerized by the bobblehead Jesus on the dashboard and by all the new sights that flashed by. My mom looked scared to death as we squeezed through impossibly small gaps in traffic and played chicken with motorbikes down one-way streets.

We zoomed past busy outdoor markets and crept by endless fruit carts piled high with bananas, mangoes, and vegetables I had never seen before. Kids sold chips at red lights and men cleaned windshields for change, jumping out of the way as the lights turned green. I loved the towering trees that filled the city and the vines that strangled their trunks. I struggled to read the billboards, catching only a few words I had learned in my one semester of Spanish. I was surprised by all the ornate churches and the black plumes that spit from tail pipes. The cacophony of Spanish music, horns, and the rumbles of thunder from above reminded me of how far I was from home. Just as we crossed Avenida 7 and my dad blurted, "A la derecha, a la derecha," the skies opened, unleashing a monsoon of rain. People scurried for cover, our driver veered right, and my view was quickly impaired by a fogged window.

The intrigue of it all instantly vanished, and I was overcome with sadness. I realized I had let my excitement distract me from the two things that I had never been distracted from before.

"I really hope Brutus and Ursula are okay," I said to my mom.

"Yeah. Me too. I hope everyone's okay," she said.

"I need to call Doris as soon as we get to the house," I said.

My dad was deep in conversation with the taxi driver but must have been listening to ours. He shifted his body to face the back seats.

"Justin. Absolutely not. You are *not* going to continue your phone addiction while we are here. You can send her an email," he said.

No one actively used email in 1997, and there was no way I was going to wait weeks to see if the bears were okay. Before I could respond, my mom spoke up.

"We'll go buy a phone card and make some calls once we have settled in," she said, completely ignoring my dad's outburst, and assuring me with a pat on my knee.

It took us an hour to arrive at a large house on the outskirts of town. It was surrounded by oversized hibiscus bushes, beautiful trees, and a fifteen-foot-tall barbed wire fence. The taxi honked a few times and a short, rotund woman hurried down the driveway to open the gate. She wore bright green pajamas, flip-flops, and lots of blush.

"Hola. Hola. Welcome." She greeted us with a big smile, waving us in under the carport.

Her name was Xenya. Her Spanish was fast, and her English was limited. My parents had agreed to rent two bedrooms in her house, and she agreed to cook for us during our stay.

She helped us bring our luggage in. It was a spacious place covered in tropical plants. There were bars on the windows but no glass, which allowed a cool breeze to pass through the house. My parents' room was connected to mine by a small bathroom and there was a hammock on the back patio.

Once we settled in, Xenya offered us lunch. We all sat at the counter overlooking the kitchen as she diced cilantro for the top of the beans and rice she had made us. She served guacamole, fried bananas, and a blended fruit drink.

"Muy bien." I pointed to the food, trying the little Spanish I knew.

I scooped a spoonful of beans and rice into my mouth and bit into a big blob of chewiness. I had never tasted anything like it and spit it out onto my plate.

"What's that?" I asked, investigating it with my spoon.

"No problemo. No problemo. Esta grasa de cerdo. Es good for you," she said.

"Ohhh. That's pig fat," my dad said, looking at me nervously.

I lost my shit. "Dad. You didn't tell her I'm vegetarian? I can't believe that I just chewed on a dead pig's fat. That is really disgusting."

While Xenya could only speak a little English, she couldn't miss my body language and my tone of voice. She asked my dad what was wrong and he explained that I was a vegetarian.

"Lo siento. I am sorry. Solamente vegetariano from now on," she promised.

I ate the fried bananas and guacamole and after lunch, my mom and I walked down a narrow sidewalk to find a phone. We dodged potholes and jumped over puddles as a steady stream of cars passed just inches from us. We walked into a small store whose front window was covered in phone card posters and lottery tickets. My mom's attempt at Spanish worked and she exchanged the equivalent of ten US dollars for a bright yellow phone card. The woman behind the counter smiled and waved us toward a phone in the front corner of the store.

I scratched the back of the card and dialed Doris. I was surprised my mom let me call her before she called our family, but I was happy.

"Doris! It's Justin." I had to talk loudly over endless honking and a guy who had stumbled into the store screaming for beer. "Are Brutus and Ursula okay?" I covered my other ear to hear her response. My mom stood by, watching for my reaction. I sighed with relief when I heard the news: Fish and Game had successfully rescued the bears from their cage, and they would spend the rest of the winter safe from the floods at a holding facility. My mom and I hugged to celebrate, and all I could do was hope that the radio station would keep bringing money into the bank account while I was gone.

Later that night at Xenya's, I unpacked my luggage and taped a photo of Brutus and one of Ursula on the wall next to my bed. I said good night to my mom, who was brushing her teeth in my doorway.

"Sweet dreams, honey," she said, trying to keep the toothpaste in her mouth.

She closed my door and I climbed under the covers. It was the first time that I would sleep in a real bed since thieves had stolen our car five years prior. There was no closet to hide in anymore. My parents were close by, the windows had bars, and we were protected by a tall barbed wire fence. I lay there and wiggled with joy about the new feelings I had. I was so far from home and felt safe in the world.

From that place of safety, I was ready to start a brand-new school. It helped that ninth grade back home had been easier than middle school and was bully-free. I started at a K–12 international school that sat on a lush hillside overlooking San Jose. My class was full of rich Costa Rican kids and a few foreigners. We all learned in English and everyone was fluent in Spanish except for three of us. Otto was from Helsinki, Kevin was from Seoul, and I represented California. We became fast friends while we were sequestered from the rest of our class during Spanish period. Our Spanish was so bad, they sent us to the elementary school Spanish teacher. We sat in child-sized chairs, surrounded by kiddy posters, and our teacher tried to get us to play silly games. She had no idea how to teach kids our age, so we spent most of the time speaking English to each other. It was really nice to get to know Otto and Kevin; they were so different from the kids I knew in America. They were so nice and were genuinely curious about my story.

School in Costa Rica was much better than my school back home. We studied Africa in geography class, the Chinese dynasties in history, and Shakespeare in English. It was a worldly and engaged place to be, but it was not the highlight of my time in Costa Rica. Weekends were! Someone had introduced me to the director of an animal sanctuary called Zoo Ave and it was just two hours away by bus from our house. On Friday of that first week, I couldn't wait to get out of school and get home so I could catch the series of buses that would take me to the zoo where I would spend the night. I was pretty nervous about the idea of traveling two hours on multiple buses in a country where I hardly spoke the language, but my dad had offered to join me on my first journey.

We jumped on a local bus that took twenty minutes to get down the hill through the busy streets of San Jose. We got to the central bus station just in time to catch the four-thirty bus to Alajuela.

"It's important you look at the front of the bus and make sure it says *directo*. See right there?" my dad said, pointing. "If you don't take the direct bus it could take you an hour and a half. The direct bus only takes forty-five minutes." I nodded, committing the information to memory for my solo trip the next week. We jumped on the bus and slinked past curious eyes, caged chickens, and stacks of shopping bags, before finally finding a seat at the back of the bus. It was a bumpy ride into Central Alajuela, and we were both a little queasy when we got off at the depot. From there, we had to catch a bus to La Garita.

"We just have to ask the driver to stop at Zoo Ave," Dad said, asking me if I knew how to make that request in Spanish.

"No!" I said, looking at him like he was crazy. I really only knew how to ask for food and where the bathroom was. He grabbed a piece of paper that was slipped into my *Lonely Planet* guidebook and read: "Puede usted parar el autobús en la Zoo Ave."

We walked down a long row of buses looking for ours. I repeated what my dad said over and over:

"Puede usted parar el autobús en la Zoo Ave."

"Puede usted parar el autobús en la Zoo Ave."

"Puede usted parar el autobús en la Zoo Ave."

A bus came rumbling up behind us—it was the La Garita bus. We both stepped aside and waved the driver down. He opened the doors and slowed just enough for us to jump on. That bus was crazier than the other. The music was louder, there were more chickens, and even more people staring at us. There wasn't a single seat available and not much standing room, either. My dad looked at me and tilted his head toward the driver, inviting me to practice.

"Hola," I yelled over the music. "Puede parar el autobús a Zoo Ave," I said, stumbling over my words.

The driver kept his eyes on the road. "¡Si, Si! Zoo Ave. No lejos." *Not far.*

I gripped the seat that my dad was holding on to as the driver accelerated out of the bus depot and out of town. The countryside was lush and green, and our driver drove like a bat out of hell down the pothole-riddled road. He swerved around dogs, cars, and cattle, slowing just enough for us to jump off in front of Zoo Ave.

The air was filled with the sound of squawking birds and a distinct smell of animals. We stepped through the gates and entered paradise. It was an amazing jungle full of trees and all sorts of wild sounds. We greeted the cashier and she radioed for Dennis, a friendly Canadian who owned Zoo Ave. He had a big beard, thick glasses, a wide-brimmed fedora, and wore khaki from head to toe. He seemed excited to have us there and launched into a tour.

"This used to be a terrible roadside zoo when I arrived here. I bought the property six years ago and turned it into a rescue and rehabilitation center. We have thirty-six acres and about two thousand animals. After you told me what you are doing for those bears, I knew you'd fit right in here," he said, patting me on the shoulder.

We walked down the lush, tree-lined path, stopping to meet a troop of monkeys who lounged in the trees high above us. "These are our spider monkeys," Dennis said. "They are my favorite. They just love swinging in the trees and getting high from the mango blossoms."

We walked past a lake full of caiman, and then stopped at a large aviary. Two large green birds perched just above our eye level. Their red bellies and long iridescent tails glimmered in the sun. "These are our quetzals," Dennis said. "Their wings were clipped, so these poor girls can't fly." Dennis began making a cooing sound toward them. "They are the rare ones who stay here. We'll release most of the other animals that live here now when they're ready."

We met monkeys, felines, birds, and animals I never knew existed. It was a magical place.

I was thrilled to learn that zoos could actually have an ethical mission, that they could treat animals with dignity and create exhibits that replicated their natural habitats. I wished Brutus and Ursula could be there with me.

Finally, Dennis opened a large fifteen-foot-tall rusted metal gate that led us to the backside of the zoo where workers prepped food. He pointed to a cluster of cages, stopping at one filled with large freshly cut tree branches. Two creatures that looked like little bears with a monkey tail scampered to the front of the cage and Dennis stuck his finger in. "This is Pepper and Lane—our kinkajous. They were raised as pets, so they are really adjusted to humans." He invited us to stick our fingers in and one nuzzled mine. It had the softest fur I had ever felt. And it had a cute little face. I was in love.

We walked past a large outdoor kitchen that smelled of fermented fruit and Dennis unlatched a door to a small, barren room. It was painted a bright aqua blue with a small bed, mosquito net, a rickety old desk, and a single bulb that hung from the ceiling. "This is where you'll be staying at night," Dennis said. The plan was for me to spend Friday and Saturday nights at the zoo, giving me two full days with all the amazing animals. It was like a dream come true.

I said goodbye to my dad, who headed back to San Jose, and soon Dennis left, too.

The keepers' house was a lonely place at night. A few geckos on the walls and a swarm of bugs were the only things that kept me company. The distant sound of howler monkeys and my homework held my attention. I lay under a thin paisley sheet, protected by the net. My pillow was doubled over as I studied a map of Africa: Mali. Morocco. Senegal. Ivory Coast. Guinea. I memorized the map, repeating the countries in my head over and over. I had a test on Monday, and I knew the only way my parents would let me volunteer at the zoo was if I kept my grades up.

It was still dark when Dennis woke me the next morning. He handed me a piece of paper that was labeled "Justin's Tasks" that explained what I would be doing. "I'm going to walk you through everything today," he said, "and then I'll set you free tomorrow."

I started reading down the list, using the light that glowed from the kitchen window. Dennis grabbed a bucket of chopped fruit.

1. *Keys are to be returned at the end of the day.*
2. *Cut mango branches for birds and monkeys.*
3. *Gather mango blossoms for spider monkeys.*
4. *Monitor mouse traps. Live mice go in the aquarium. Dead mice in the freezer.*
5. *Sun boas. Clean their cages.*

"Who is 'Boas?'" I asked, hoping it was another kinkajou. Boy was I wrong. Boas meant boa constrictors, and sunning them meant they would slither up my arm, over my shoulders, and then I was supposed to stand in the sun with them for thirty minutes. We walked over to the snakes' aquarium and Dennis popped open the top. "This is Skull and Pierce. They are used to being handled. You just have to be careful when you stick your hand in to get them. Make sure it's behind their head so they don't mistake it for food."

I thought he must have been kidding me. "What do you mean mistake you for food?" I asked. My heart pounded and my mind raced. I was terribly afraid of reptiles, particularly snakes. I couldn't imagine sticking my hand in their tank, let alone letting them slither around my neck.

"Don't worry. They are all old pets, so they are really docile. They just can't see that well," Dennis said. I wanted to make a good impression, so I didn't say how I felt.

The sun's rays hit the top of the trees and created a beautiful pink hue in the sky as we walked down the verdant paths. I glanced up every few seconds to watch where we were going and continued reading the list:

6. *Check the iguana exhibit for tunnels. Fill any tunnels found.*

7. *Cut bamboo for Monkey Enrichment.*

8. *Hang out with Monday.*

"Who is Monday?" I asked Dennis, pointing to number eight on the list. I was worried it might have been a *"really docile"* alligator. "You'll meet Monday later. You've got to check for tunnels now," he said, pointing to a small stone fence that stood between me and about one hundred green iguanas. Many of them were three to four feet long. I reluctantly listened to Dennis and jumped into the exhibit. The hoards of lizards seemed unfazed by my presence, but the opposite was true for me. I felt surrounded. I tried to control my breathing. Everywhere I looked there were big, green, scary lizards staring at me with their beady eyes. I couldn't stop thinking about the Dilophosaurus from *Jurassic Park*, the one dinosaur that had kept me up at night. I was just waiting for one of the iguanas to spit venom in my eyes, for me to topple over, to get eaten alive.

Dennis handed a shovel to me over the fence. "Just head to the back of the exhibit and make sure to push the dirt back into the tunnels they've dug up."

I really didn't like the idea of walking through this enclosure of dinosaurs, but I did it anyway. As I walked slowly to the rear of the exhibit, hoping not to disturb anything, I saw about a dozen holes.

"There are a ton of holes back here," I yelled, just loud enough for Dennis to hear.

"You just cover them up," he casually yelled back to me.

I moved quickly to fill each hole so I could get out of there. I finished covering one hole, and then another, and another—and then it happened, my worst nightmare.

Just as I finished scooting a big pile of dirt back into a large escape tunnel, a huge lizard came charging in my direction. It moved fast, it was big, and it looked mad. Its eyes were fixated on me. Its neck frill was extended. Its mouth gaped open. It's four-foot-long tail whipped back and forth. Its body was tense like an angry pit bull. I was under attack. I screamed bloody murder, which made all the other lizards near me scatter, knocking my assailant off course, giving me just enough time to jump onto the stone wall and over the backside of the exhibit to safety.

"Are you okay?" Dennis asked, jogging around the perimeter to meet me.

"I thought you said they were vegetarians," I cried.

"They are!" he said, noticing the angry male. "I should have told you they can be territorial during breeding season."

"Well, I should have told you that I'm scared to death of reptiles," I said.

I was glad that I survived the iguana attack, and that it happened when it did. The adrenaline of it all boosted my confidence enough that I could be honest with Dennis. That honesty helped me get exactly what I wanted at Zoo Ave. I told Dennis that I had been studying mammal enrichment and that I could really help entertain the monkeys with the techniques I had learned. He was curious and asked me what I would do.

"I noticed that there was a bamboo patch near the mango orchard. I could chop bamboo into sections, drill holes in it, and stuff them full of mealworms for the squirrel monkeys," I said, rattling off that and ten other ideas I had read about in my magazines back home.

Dennis was impressed and made me the weekend monkey keeper. I was tasked with making sure that they were fed in the morning and entertained throughout the day. I would start by cutting over thirty pounds of fruit and lugging two big pails across the zoo for the five species. I would spend the afternoon sawing mango tree branches for them to browse on and I would make puzzles for them to play with.

The squirrel monkeys were always playful and loved bouncing off my head. The capuchins, despite living in three acres of jungle, really hated captivity and were always poised to attack. The spider monkeys were mischievous, regularly pulling my glasses off my face with their tails and doing other naughty things.

By far my favorite time of the day was hanging out with Monday. He was a howler monkey whose mom had died. I would tromp through the back trails to the patch of forest where the howlers lived and yell his name at the top of my lungs.

"Mooooooondaaaaaaay," I would call with a deep voice. He would always come scampering to the gate. I would open it just enough for him to crawl out, up my leg, and into my arms where I would have a towel waiting for him.

He would look into my eyes, grinding his little teeth and clinging tightly as we walked around the back trails of the zoo. He didn't seem to like the capuchins, who would shake the fence as we passed, so we would take the long way to the mango orchard, where we'd spend an hour or so just hanging out. He usually wanted to stay close but sometimes he would feel adventurous, bounding up a tree where he would perch by himself, keeping a close eye on me. I felt so at home hidden away among the mango trees, their sweet smell filling the air, meditating with Monday.

The slow pace of those weekend jungle escapes helped me and Monday build a bond that I had never experienced with an animal before. I could feel his warmth, his little hands that fit around my finger, and his tail that he would wrap tightly around my arm. I experienced his range of emotions and my own. I loved him like I loved Brutus and Ursula, but a thick-gauged fence had kept me from connecting with the bears the way I was able to connect with Monday. I imagined the bears would have been as gentle and sweet as young Monday was with me, enjoying the sounds of the forest and following me, as he did, when it was time to go.

In the evening, I would tuck Monday away in a cage in the zoo's warm nursery where he would sleep and then I would have to say goodbye. I was always sad when Sunday afternoon rolled around because it meant I had to return to the realities of the big city—where quizzes, writing assignments, and long hours of sitting awaited me.

And before I returned to the San Jose bus depot where my parents would pick me up, I would face the bumpy and challenging rides across the countryside. Back and forth I went each weekend, dreading the trips at first but slowly getting the hang of them. My Spanish improved, I learned to dodge taxis crossing the road, I accepted that some bus drivers would refuse to stop when I requested, and all the staring eyes became the norm. I felt my confidence growing like a muscle.

Charging dinosaurs and long bus rides weren't the only fears that I faced living in Costa Rica. On some weekends my parents and I would go on adventures that forced me out of my comfort zone in some way. We did night hikes in the jungle where we discovered glowworms, dodged bats, and crossed active nests of tarantulas. We got pulled over and interrogated by police with automatic weapons in Guatemala. By far the most intense experience we had was a short trip to Cuba, where we risked being thrown in jail.

In the '90s, any Americans who stepped foot on the communist island could be convicted of trading with the enemy, face years in prison, and pay massive fines. There were no flights from the US to Cuba but living in Costa Rica meant we could fly there directly. I became obsessed with the idea of experiencing a culture so different from capitalism and I loved the idea of going somewhere our government didn't want us. After endlessly nagging my parents, they agreed to risk the trip and spend a week there during my spring break.

We boarded a Havana-bound flight in an old Soviet plane without water to drink or air-conditioning to bring down the uncomfortable temperatures. Everyone on the plane clapped when we took off and cheered when we landed. Our taxi driver from the airport was a doctor by trade, who said he made more money working in tourism. Billboards that would have promoted fast food and soda on the freeways back home instead promoted communism. *Viva Cuba Libre, Todo por la Revolución, Batalla de Ideas* the colorful signs read as we sped past images of Fidel Castro, Che Guevara, and a toothless Uncle Sam. Those billboards, the old cars, and decaying architecture reminded me of how far we were from the US and its endless reminders to consume. We walked into local shops with barely any food on the shelves, and as we drove across the island, people waved from their porches and would surround our car when we pulled into town, eager to know our story.

There was a warmth about the people—their big smiles, their willingness to invite us into their homes, and the way they wrapped their arms around each other. It was all so refreshing and different from the way people interacted in the US. We had forty-eight rolls of irresistibly soft toilet paper back home; in Cuba they would cut up and crumple pieces of old math homework to do the job. Our neighbors in California would open their garage doors with remotes, pull their cars in, and never say hello to each other. People in Cuba offered my parents swigs of rum on white-sand beaches and kids taught me how to jump from cliffs into watering holes on our jungle hikes. We saw them gather, eat, laugh, and dance in the streets together, celebrating life and each other. It made me wonder what really mattered and why our government would want to hide such joy.

The week in Cuba was like nothing I had ever experienced and like no place I had ever been. I was mesmerized by it all and surprised by how quickly the week went by. The night before we were to fly back to Costa Rica, my parents and I shared a small room in a hotel with three twin-sized beds pushed together to fit. This left only a small path to the bathroom and just enough space at the foot of our beds for our laughably large suitcases.

"Justin, this was a really good idea," my mom said.

"I'm glad you nagged us to go," my dad added as we all fell asleep.

The next morning, I woke up to him saying something equally as strange.

"Where are our bags?" he asked.

"They're at the foot of the bed," my mom said.

"No, they're not," he said.

I put my glasses on and sat up just as my mom shrieked, "Oh my God! They're gone."

In the middle of the night, someone had come into our room and stolen almost everything. I flashed back to the times I had woken up terrified by the thought of thieves in California. This time—when it had really happened, when we knew that strangers would have had to crawl over us to steal our things—was different. I was grateful. It was a new feeling for me. Rather than being scared of what had happened, I was grateful I had slept through the ordeal and that we were all okay. I got up and calmly walked with my dad to the front desk. Within thirty minutes at least twenty police had arrived at the hotel; within an hour a sniffer dog had found the thieves' trail; and by the time we left for the airport, a very interesting story had unfolded.

The thieves had driven up a trail and walked down a path behind our bungalow, which sat on the edge of the hotel property. The police guessed that they had pumped sleeping gas into our room before they entered. That explained why we would have slept through it all and why my dad felt especially drowsy; he had been sleeping just inches from the cut screen and broken shutter we discovered. These well-resourced thieves took our clothes and our money but left our passports, plane tickets, a change of clothing, and the keys to our rental car. We were lucky we could leave the country without a problem.

I left Cuba without a suitcase, but I boarded that plane back to Costa Rica with something much better than a bag full of clothes. I was happy to be alive. I was grateful for my parents. I hoped whoever ended up with our clothes enjoyed them. I was thankful that we had the means to buy new things and that we had enough money to go to faraway places to get robbed in the first place.

When the school year ended in June, I said goodbye to Otto and Kevin. Summer meant more time at the zoo for me and more time for my family to explore Costa Rica together. We went all over, practicing our much-improved Spanish with the locals. We met fellow travelers, people from the Bribri tribe, sloths, stingrays, and pit vipers. We swam in the Caribbean and bodysurfed in the Pacific. We hiked into many jungles and spent much of the summer covered in mosquito and fire ant bites. We enjoyed home-cooked meals and each other's company.

As the new school year back in the States inched closer, I had to say goodbye to Monday and all the animals at Zoo Ave. My mom and dad joined me for my last day there, filming my daily routine with a borrowed camcorder. I chopped my last bucket of papaya for the monkeys; let Lane, the kinkajou, pee on me one last time; and trained the new volunteer keeper. "She's the new keeper. It's her first day," I whispered to my mom with a sense of pride. I got such a boost of confidence from knowing that I had learned enough to train someone almost twice my age.

I was proud of the work I had done at the zoo, but I was proud of more than just that. Something had happened to me in those seven months. A lot of things had happened to me. I braved a new school and met new friends. I got covered in mud, poop, urine, and lots of mango sap. I crossed dangerous riverways and survived knockout gases. I traveled solo and learned to appreciate my parents more than I ever had. I faced my fears and realized that whether it was a thief, a lizard, or a communication barrier, I would be okay.

When the time came to get on that plane back to California, I wasn't sad or anxious or worried. I was ready to see Brutus and Ursula, start a new school year, and face whatever would come my way.

I flipped on my bedroom light after seven months away and it was as if time had stood still. My Rolodex sat perfectly aligned at the top right of my desk, the same PETA posters adorned my walls, and my bed was made just as I had left it. I threw my bags down, brushed my teeth, and then I noticed something *was* different. My ceiling was lower. I was confused at first and then it hit me. It wasn't that the ceiling was lower; I had grown taller—and it seemed like quite a bit taller. I crawled into bed, trying to anticipate what else might have changed while I was gone. I couldn't wait to wake up the next morning to go see the bears, see how much money the radio station had raised, and check in with the people at the Folsom Zoo about the new enclosure.

I was convinced that Roseville must have improved the bears' conditions while I was gone. I figured that at least the floor of their cage would be covered in dirt.

Boy was I wrong.

Absolutely nothing had been done to improve the bears' conditions, and Brutus and Ursula looked sadder than ever. I kicked myself. Why would I have expected Roseville to do anything for the bears without my nagging? A wave of guilt washed over me, and then I got angry. I had always known improving the bears' cage was the right thing to do, but my time at Zoo Ave taught me something else: It wasn't that hard to treat animals well in captivity, or anywhere, for that matter. You just had to give them ample space, the foods they would naturally eat, and re-create what life was like in the wild. I had known these things in my heart but confirmed them by working with all the amazing animals in Costa Rica.

Our stop at the bank was just as pathetic. The radio station had only raised ten thousand dollars while I was gone. Little did I know that I had handed the project to their sales team, who spent those seven months using the bears to sell ads. "Come on down to Hair Town this Saturday for the Roseville Bear Cut-a-Thon. We'll donate a percentage of revenue to help build Brutus and Ursula's new home at the Folsom Zoo," one commercial said. The bears got almost nothing from the deal.

Luckily, my visit to Folsom Zoo was a whole other story. The distant screams of a peacock and the wafting smell of poop sent me back to my dreamy days at Zoo Ave. While the animals at Folsom didn't have ample space like the animals in Costa Rica, the staff were deeply committed to doing everything they could to help them live well. As we walked through the zoo, a family recognized me from the news and thanked me for being a good role model. It felt nice to be recognized and warmly welcomed by all the zoo staff.

"Justin, you're back!" one of the keepers exclaimed from the inside of Vixen and Cole's exhibit—two friendly red foxes rescued from a fur farm. As she spread kibble around their cage to encourage foraging, she asked me a ton of questions about Costa Rica and my experiences at Zoo Ave. Then she broke some exciting news. "The architects finished the designs and there is a model of the bears' new home in the office." She finished with the foxes and took me and my dad to see it.

I was so happy to see things were progressing and to study the miniature version of the bears' future home. There were tiny trees that held a bear hammock, and the floor of the model was sprinkled with dirt and tufts of native plants. There was a small pool with a waterfall that would be big enough to fit both Brutus and Ursula. Their evening quarters would have heated floors and big piles of straw for a cozy night's sleep. It was incredibly humbling to see what the future held— and to realize there was still at least $100,000 to raise before workers could even think about breaking ground. The anger I felt seeing the bears' cage in Roseville and the stagnation I sensed at seeing the bank account total had disappeared. I was fired up and ready to ensure that the prototype came to life—and that it happened quickly.

I began to make a plan for getting some media to come to town, reconnecting with all my animal rights friends, and filling that bank account. I wanted to help the bears, but I also wanted to take advantage of my new-found confidence. My head was full of new ideas, I was proud of all my travels, and seven months away helped me appreciate Sacramento in a way I never had. Seeing Sybil helped me confirm that I had changed.

"Look at you," she said as I walked into her office. She struggled to get up from her chair to give me a hug. "My, oh my. You're like a different person." She grabbed my shoulders in amazement.

I wanted to tell her everything, but an hour was only enough time to share some highlights and to gush about how much closer I felt with my parents.

"We haven't fought for so long."

"How'd *that* happened?" she asked, giving me a look like she never thought she'd hear those words.

"I think it's me. I *feel* like a different person."

"How are you going to keep it up?"

She was right. I needed to keep things good with my parents, and expensive phone bills had been one of our biggest fights. I called our local telephone company and asked if they would donate a phone line and cover my bills.

"In all my time here, I have never known the company to donate a phone line," the head of marketing told me. "But your story convinced them, and we can have someone out there later this week to install the line."

I started tenth grade feeling pretty optimistic about everything. My classmates' suburban routines had nothing on the world I had just explored. I didn't feel like I was better than them. I just felt above all their petty bullshit.

I didn't care about how cool the jocks thought they were, how cliquey the cheerleaders acted, or how serious student council took everything. Feeling above something, however, was not the same as feeling part of it, and the second I stepped into second-period Spanish class, something profound happened that made me feel included in a way I never had before.

My teacher was Ms. Milano. She was one of those over-the-top Spanish teachers who exaggerated every word that came out of her mouth and insisted that we spoke Spanish exclusively for the entire period. Right before the bell rang, this kid named Nick waltzed in. He was one of the star football players who was always surrounded by a flock of cheerleaders. His backpack was hanging over his shoulder and he acted like he owned the place. Everyone seemed to drool over him. The way his navy polo clung tightly to his muscular body and his Abercrombie hat sat backward on his head *was* kinda hot. He completely ignored Ms. Milano's greeting and pointed at one of the other football players who was sitting sideways in his chair. "What's up, bro?" Nick said, giving his friend a nod. Like a bad movie, he winked at one of the girls in the third row, who giggled, and then he headed toward the last available desk, which happened to be directly behind me.

I was excited about Spanish class because I understood everything that Ms. Milano said. I just knew I was going to crush that class. We started that day by conjugating future subjunctives out loud. "Yo hablare," we all said in unison. "Tu hablares." Just as we got to el, ella, usted, the class said "hablare" and Nick said something else. Four words that hit me like a ton of bricks and made my heart race. "This is so gay," he said. I had spent so many years hearing people use "gay" as a put-down and, now that I had an idea that that was how I identified, I couldn't just sit there in silence. I spun around in my seat and locked eyes with Nick. "That's offensive," I said, in English. "If you don't like future subjunctives just say you don't like them. You don't have to call them gay."

He looked surprised by my reaction. "Are you a fag or something?" he asked.

The exchange was loud enough that Ms. Milano stopped the class. "¿Qué es el problema aqui?" she asked.

A kid who I had never met answered her question. "Nick just called your lesson gay and then just called him"—he pointed at me—"a fag. It's making me really uncomfortable."

I piped in. "He's right and it's making me uncomfortable, too."

Ms. Milano's cheery demeanor quickly shifted and then she broke her own rule "I won't accept that language in this class," she said, locking eyes with Mr. Abercrombie, who had turned bright red from embarrassment. She then addressed the entire class. "I don't want to hear any hurtful things in this classroom and if I do, you're done. Tolerancia Cero. That's Zero Tolerance." She walked to the phone on the wall next to her desk and picked it up. "I need student services to come to room 214 for an escort to the office."

"Ohhhhhhh." The low rumbling of student reactions filled the room. Ms. Milano started filling out a yellow piece of paper and glanced in Nick's direction. "Pack your things up. You can explain yourself to the vice principal." I turned back and flashed a satisfactory smirk his way, and then I caught eyes with the other kid who had spoken up with me. He gave me a big smile. It was pure joy.

Nick was escorted out and Spanish class returned to normal. I was so distracted and happy when the bell finally rang for lunch. "Hasta mañana," Ms. Milano exclaimed, waving at the class as we exited.

"Muchas gracias, Profesora," I said to her as we walked out.

"Con mucho gusto," she responded. "I am sorry."

Once we got out the door, my stomach dropped from excitement. "Hey. What's your name?" the kid who had spoken up asked me. "I'm James. That was awesome in there!"

"I'm Justin. He would have gotten away with it if you hadn't backed me up. Thanks for that."

"So, are you?" James asked. "Gay, I mean?"

I didn't even hesitate before answering. I was, and I knew it, and I was ready to be honest about it. "Hell yeah I am. Are you?"

"Come with me," James said, grabbing my hand and pulling me toward the cafeteria.

Laguna Creek was situated on a sprawling outdoor campus with a large grassy knoll at the center that butted up against the large cafeteria. The lunch room accommodated 1600 students and their daily fix of fries, nachos, chicken patties, soda, and rotating pans of slop. We walked through the wide corridors, following the crowds toward the grease. I had no idea where James was taking me. "I haven't seen you around here before," he said, as we squeezed past a group of loud cheerleaders taking up half of the sidewalk practicing a cheer. We walked across the squishy grass toward the side of the lunchroom building where a group of girls was hanging out. Two sat cross-legged, staring into each other's eyes, while the others stood in a small circle talking.

"Hey, y'all," James said, getting everyone's attention. "This is Justin. He's one of us." Everyone welcomed me and James went around and introduced everyone. "This is Shamona." She was tall, thick, and beautiful. She wore huge bell bottom jeans and a tight Nirvana shirt that showed off her curves. I went to shake her hand and she deflected it and leaned in for a long hug. She released me, held my shoulders, and looked me in the eyes. "Welcome, friend."

The feeling of overwhelming acceptance swirled inside of me. It was like nothing I had felt before, especially at school. James continued to introduce the others. "This is Kathy and Christina. These two are inseparable. I have never seen one without the other," James joked. Kathy was the shortest in the group with tight, ripped, black jeans; big brunette bangs; and thick, black eyeliner. Christina wore a short, red plaid skirt that landed just above her knees and with ripped fishnets. Her tight blond curls bounced in excitement. Kathy and Christina both hugged me at the same time. "Group hug!" Christina screamed out as James and Shamona joined in. "They call us the Cutters and the Queers," James said to me as he grabbed Kathy's arm and showed me tons of small scars that ran up her forearm like parallel railroad tracks. "She's the cutter in the group."

Kathy rolled her eyes and jerked her arm out of James's hand. "You like cock. I like adrenaline rushes," she said, glaring at James. He dropped his mouth open, acting like he was insulted, then laughed and nuzzled her. "You know I love you, girl," he said. He turned back to me and whispered just loud enough for her to hear: "Some of us are gay and some of us are suicidal."

We plopped down on the grass and he made loud kissing noises at the two seated girls. "This is Erinn and Sarah. Our little love birds." They unlocked from a kiss and laughed at James's introduction. Sarah looked more embarrassed than Erinn. She had spiky red hair and lipstick to match. Erinn wore a collared shirt tucked into khakis. She radiated confidence. Her only feminine feature was her perfect A-line bob. She adjusted herself into a kneeling position, giving me a long hug. We lost our balance and she fell onto me and we both erupted into laughter. After years of longing for real friends, her hug and the belly laughter that followed gave me that first taste of belonging that I had never felt before. Sarah joined our pile and their weight pushed down on my chest and legs. We just laughed as the slightly wet grass soaked into my jeans. It felt like a dream come true. In that moment, I knew it was going to be a good year. We untangled from our pile and Erinn wanted to know what happened in Spanish class. Everyone joined our circle to hear the story.

"That is so awesome," Erinn said, giving James and me high fives. "Other than Goldie, all the staff are pretty supportive of us LGBTQ kids," Sarah said.

"What's LGBTQ?" I asked. Sarah grabbed a small rainbow flag that was sticking out of the side pocket of her backpack. "Lesbian, Gay, Bisexual, Transgender, and Queer." She waved the flag, completely ignoring the naivete of my question. It was the first time I had ever heard those letters together. From the corner of my eye, I saw one of the campus monitors marching in our direction.

"Speak of the devil," James said under his breath. Sarah and Erinn quickly unlatched their hands and scooted away from each other. I wasn't sure what was happening, but the mood of the group quickly changed.

Goldie had a head full of braids, tight stretch pants, and an oversized gold 49ers jacket that matched her front tooth and the tips of her long nails.

"It looks like you're finally learning the rules, ladies." She ignored the rest of the group, focusing her attention on Erinn and Sarah. "Maybe we can be friends this year," she said, holding her ear up to her walkie talkie and quickly darting away from our circle.

"She's the worst," James said under his breath.

"What's up with her?" I asked.

"She is a homophobe. That's what's up," Sarah blurted out. "Anytime she sees me and Erinn holding hands she harasses the shit out of us."

"She threatened us with detention every other day last year," Erinn said.

"She's just jealous of you two. She wants a piece of that beautiful ass," James said, raising an eyebrow at Erinn, who mimed gagging at the thought.

Laguna Creek High School, and much of the surrounding neighborhood, was an amazingly diverse place. "One of the most diverse schools in the most diverse cities in the nation," the principal would tout. I was raised seeing faces, hearing languages, and experiencing perspectives different from my own. I was a middle-class, white kid who had spent my entire life in classrooms, playgroups, and gatherings where there was no noticeable difference between the number of Asian, Black, white, and Latinx kids. Everyone always called it a melting pot, but it felt more like a fruit salad to me. We all had our own sweet, unique flavors but we were better together. My new high school crew was no exception. We all had different tastes in music, diverse skin colors, and came from an array of economic statuses. Our fashion senses and family histories were different, but we shared a common bond as outcasts. After years of flying solo, it felt good to be in with the outsiders.

I got pretty comfortable being out at school and decided that it was time to tell my family. I knew my brother had a few gay friends and I recalled a time when I was twelve and he chased a kid down the street for calling me a fag. I figured he would be cool with it, and that he could then help me figure out how to tell Mom and Dad. Mom worked the late shift and Dad taught night classes on Wednesdays, so it was a perfect night to invite him over for dinner.

When I heard him jiggle the keys to our front door, my stomach turned. He walked into the kitchen, still in his uniform from work, and gave me a big hug. He smelled like the typical shift at the restaurant—a mix of garlic butter and salsa. He told me about his nightmare boss and about a drunk guy who had vomited all over the side of the patio. I cut him off midstory.

"Shane. I have something to tell you." I couldn't keep it in any longer.

"I'm all ears, bro. What's up?"

"I'm gay," I said

As those words rolled off my lips, I completely lost control. My vision went blurry. It felt like I was wading through warm molasses waiting for his response. Everything slowed. I flashed to a memory of him punching through a wall during one of our many fights and hoped I hadn't misjudged him; I hoped he would support me.

"Justin. I love you." He gave me a huge hug and didn't let go. "I will always support you, no matter what."

I was really happy that my brother was so cool with it, and it was such a relief that at last someone in my family knew my secret. I hoped that my parents would be just as supportive.

I emptied a small pack of parmesan cheese into the pot of ravioli I'd just prepared and evenly distributed the pasta onto two plates.

"So…Mom and Dad don't know?"

"I haven't told them. How do you think they will take it?"

"I think they will be cool. Dad will probably take it better than Mom."

"Why do you say that?"

"Two words: yellow highlighter." He looked at me and raised his eyebrows.

My mom was a nurse and certain things came home with her. A job that requires you to wash your hands forty times a shift can make you leery of some things. We were taught to hold our breath if someone sneezed in public, she would bust out mini alcohol wipes to scrub restaurant tables to show us how dirty they actually were, and from a young age, I would come home to articles clipped from the newspaper sitting on our dinner table covered with bright yellow highlighter.

"Hey Teenagers, You're Vulnerable."

"Warning for Today's Teens about AIDS."

"Stricken Teen Warns of AIDS."

I had read the horror stories and absorbed all the warnings; I honestly knew more about the hazards of HIV then I knew about the details of sex. So, my brother had a point. Being raised in the middle of the AIDS epidemic and coming out to my overprotective mother might be a challenge.

"We all love you so much. It's going to be okay. It just may take some time for Mom," he reassured me.

I talked a lot with Erinn and Sarah about coming out, too. We had become fast friends and did almost everything together. While the three of us always hung out, Erinn and I got super close. She taught me what true friendship looked like and we quickly became besties. We spent every lunch period together, went to the movies, read magazines at the bookstore, hung at the mall, walked downtown, and talked on the phone for hours. She was comfortable getting naked in front of me when she got out of the shower and we'd poop with the door open like it was nothing. When she heard that I had never kissed anyone, she tackled me to the ground and insisted she be the first.

She loved all my weird quirks and thought it was so bizarre I didn't know anything about music. Other than Michael Jackson's *Dangerous* album, I had never been that into music. I usually just listened to what my parents played: Jefferson Airplane, Joni Mitchell, Three Dog Night—ex-hippie shit. I was clueless when it came to anything modern. "Do you know who Björk is? What about Ani DiFranco? How about Tori Amos?" Erinn would ask, rattling off her favorites. I didn't know any of them and when she insisted I listen, I wasn't a fan. It just wasn't my kind of music. Nothing was, until the day a kid in my English class asked me a question that would turn me into a raving music fan.

"Do you like the Spice Girls?"

For a minute I thought they were just another folksy, emo group, but then he slid their CD across my desk. I opened the case and flipped through the booklet. The Spice Girls were like nothing I had seen before. Their fashion sense was out of this world and they looked like they were having more fun than anyone on earth. Luckily, the kid had his Discman and let me listen as we left class. "Slam it to the left / If you're havin' a good time / Shake it to the right / If ya know that you feel fine."

It was so catchy and made me want to dance. Kids rushed around us, but I stood there, holding those headphones tightly over my ears moving my body to what would become the soundtrack for the rest of high school. I felt like Sporty, Ginger, Scary, Posh, and Baby were all singing to me. I was surrounded by new friends and getting comfortable with my identity. Their messages of camaraderie, self-love, and girl power were exactly what I needed. I loved their music, their unabashed confidence, and their over-the-top sense of style. They inspired me to be free, to spice things up, and ditch my bland wardrobe.

What started with a few Hawaiian shirts from the thrift store quickly turned into a full-fledged makeover. Mom didn't want to help me cultivate my new style, but my dad did. He would take me to the mall and let me buy anything I wanted—and anything meant everything shiny. Polyester pants, rayon shirts, and anything that popped. I started dressing like no other kid at school. My new wardrobe did not define me, but it helped me express how colorful I felt on the inside—and helped me rebel against the suburban sea of jeans and collared shirts. Between the shimmer of my pants, my endless singing and dancing, and my frequent outbursts of "Blah, blah, Girl Power," I had become a real spectacle. I was happy and my whole life felt like it sparkled.

When CBS *This Morning* agreed to come to Roseville to do a piece on the bears, and I received an invitation to be the guest of honor at the Genesis Awards in Hollywood, it felt like the sparkles in my personal life were rubbing off on the bears, too. I began to prepare for those events, trying to figure out how to leverage them to get more money for Ursula and Brutus.

One day, not long before the CBS cameras showed up, my mom and I were driving back from the grocery store and she asked me about my day. "Sarah and Erinn got detention for kissing today," I said. "The boys can kiss their girlfriends all they want, but the second two girls kiss, the hall narcs go nuts. It's stupid."

"What about you, honey," Mom asked. "Do you like men or women?"

The question hung in the air for a split second. I had been waiting for this moment and hoped that openly talking about my friends would inspire it. I didn't want to simply announce to my parents that I was gay; I wanted them to see it—to see *me*. I wasn't sure how they would respond. I knew they loved me, but Ellen hadn't come out yet and being gay was just not that culturally acceptable. "I'm attracted to guys," I said, as nonchalantly as I could.

Her eyes stayed locked on the road. She was silent for what felt like ten minutes. She took in a deep breath and then she said something that shouldn't have surprised me.

"I love you, honey," she said.

Soon my dad knew, too, and I called my brother to tell him he was right.

"They were both really cool with it," I said. "Mom asked if she was ever going to have grandbabies, so she might be struggling a little more than Dad."

"She loves you so much. Adjusting expectations can take some time," he told me.

When the CBS crew showed up, my mom seemed to have adjusted pretty well and we finally had something in common.

"Isn't he handsome?" she whispered, referring to Manuel Gallegos, the reporter who had flown in from LA to cover the story. His camera crew set up lights in our living room and he stood there watching with his hands on his hips like a superhero. He wore khakis instead of a cape and my mom and I stared from the kitchen. He was handsome, tall, and had beautifully radiant skin. His hair was nicely combed and he had a dreamy five o'clock shadow. His chiseled face, nice smile, and deep voice were perfect for TV.

It was a little weird that my mom and I were ogling at the same guy, but I appreciated she had asked me if I thought he was handsome. It was a small gesture, but it felt like something a friend would do. It was the first time she acknowledged my desires and it made me feel like she had heard me and accepted me.

I was happy for that special moment together in the kitchen and I was excited to spend two days with Manuel. I hoped that the national appearance would inspire money to rain down on Ursula and Brutus and help me see the light at the end of that $100,000 tunnel.

Manuel Gallegos wasn't just handsome; he was smart, and he knew the power he held as a national correspondent at CBS. He asked me what he could do to help the bears and I had a simple message I wanted him to convey: we need the city to improve the bears' conditions and we need money so we can move them. Manuel promised to do his best, and he delivered. When the bears and I topped the eight a.m. hour of CBS *This Morning* and viewers heard my plea, Gallegos added his own voice to the effort. "Since our visit," he said, as he wrapped his story live from the LA studios of CBS, "Roseville City Administrators have agreed to add some enrichment like soil and trees to the bears' cage, but of course the big objective is to move them."

I was surprised and skeptical about the city's promise, but a phone call confirmed that Roseville had indeed begun planning an extension of the bears' cage that would include new logs and a layer of dirt. I couldn't believe that something I had spent two years fighting for had happened after a single call from Manuel. Maybe it was his deep voice or maybe the endless media coverage had worn the city down. Either way, it felt like good progress—and city officials were not the only people he charmed. For weeks afterward, thousands of dollars flowed into the bank from people all over the country who saw the story.

After that flood of donations slowed to a trickle, there was still $90,000 to raise. I figured Hollywood was swimming in money and as a guest at the Genesis Awards that year, I planned to take full advantage of my access to that room full of stars. The Genesis Awards celebrated media outlets and actors who advocated for animal rights and I was that year's guest of honor. I took out an ad in the program that featured a photo of Brutus and Ursula and planned to talk to as many people as I could during the event.

The ceremony began that night with a dramatic drum-roll that you'd expect from the Academy Awards. I stood up from our table as I heard my name and the spotlight shined on me to a roaring applause. It felt good to stand in that room full of famous faces, but what happened after the ceremony is what really mattered. As people were getting up from their seats and mingling, I started networking like crazy, telling anyone I could about the bears. I talked with Tippi Hedren, starlet of Hitchcock's *The Birds*; Pierce Brosnan who was James Bond at the time; Kevin Nealon, who was on *Saturday Night Live*; Amanda Plummer from Tarantino's *Pulp Fiction*; Oleg Cassini, the fashion designer who dressed Jacqueline Kennedy; and Linda Blair, whose head spun in *The Exorcist*.

I told each one of them about the bears and they all congratulated me but said they couldn't help—everyone except Linda. She became a huge supporter and sent me boxes and boxes full of autographed photos and other memorabilia from her Hollywood friends. We'd talk on the phone every few weeks and we even made shirts that said, "*Brutus and Ursula's conditions make my head spin*," with a photo of Linda's head spinning. I teamed up with Folsom Zoo and we auctioned off all that memorabilia at a fundraiser that brought in thousands of dollars. Someone actually spent two grand on an old, tattered pair of slippers from Martin Sheen who had autographed them with a silver marker, one addressed to Ursula and the other to Brutus.

The pace at which the money was flowing in had quickened, but it wasn't fast enough for me. Another winter was on its way and I was worried the bears might not survive another flood. There was still $80,000 left to raise and I decided that Roseville needed to step up. Vern Fernsby had retired as mayor but was still on the council. The new mayor must have been warned not to share her home phone number with me, but luckily, she was incredibly responsive whenever I called her office. She seemed well aware of the friends I had made in the media and wanted to do right by Brutus and Ursula. I started to pester her with a new request and a sound bite for the media: "Make it happen for the bears."

After a month or so of repetitive calls and other politicking, a resolution to fund the rest of the project landed on the agenda of a Roseville council meeting. What that meant is that in one evening, the campaign might be fully funded. I was over the moon about the news but learned there was a catch: the vote required *every single council member* and the mayor to vote yes. A single no vote meant the proposal was dead in the water.

I picked up the phone and called all my contacts at all the media outlets in Sacramento. They had spent two years covering the bears one way or another, so there wasn't much explaining to do. "Meet me in the parking lot next to city hall at six p.m.," I told each of them, explaining the gravity of the vote. Sure enough, on that important day, there were four TV trucks waiting for me in the parking lot. Every single local station and newspaper had sent a reporter and cameraperson to cover the vote. When I got out of the van with Mom and Dad, it was like a media mob I had never experienced. I explained the plan and gave each reporter a five-minute interview.

The vote was one of the first agenda items, so I gave the council five minutes to settle in and then swung the doors of the chamber open. I was surrounded by six camerapeople who filmed my entrance, and I was trailed by a gaggle of reporters and my parents. The chamber was so packed there was hardly even standing room and everyone's attention turned toward the doors as we stormed in. The council members looked shocked, which was exactly what I had hoped for. I figured if any of them dared to vote no, they would have to do it on the evening news for all to see.

As the council discussed the resolution and opened the floor for public comment, I quickly learned that almost everyone in that room was there for Brutus and Ursula. One after another, people stood up in support of the bears.

"Make us proud," one woman said.

"It's the right thing to do," another commented.

The passion I heard in their voices touched me and I was moved to see the bears had inspired so many people to show up and speak out.

I was the last to stand at that podium before that big vote and paused long enough for the cameras to settle into their positions. "People all over the country know Brutus and Ursula now. Their story has inspired people to write checks, send letters, make calls, and pack council meetings. You are each just one word away from helping the bears live a better life. Tonight, all eyes are on you to make the right decision. I trust you will make it happen for the bears."

I stood at the podium as the city manager called for a vote. The room was silent in anticipation and the cameras turned to the council members for that pivotal moment. There was one yes and then another and then another, each yes vote inspiring a rustling in the crowd. Vote by vote, the yeses continued around the semicircle. In a curious twist of fate, the final vote sat with Vern Fernsby. After my countless interruptions to his family meals and those early morning calls I had made to his house, I figured he must have hated me. I had no idea how he'd vote. I was scared he was going to let his ego get in the way and ruin everything, but I hoped the shame of the national media attention—and the number of angry calls he fielded—had gotten through to him. In that moment, as his name was called, he held all the power. Brutus and Ursula's future was in his hands. I held my breath and he paused just long enough as if to communicate that he was in on the melodrama.

"Yes."

The crowd erupted in cheers and the cameras swung back to capture my reaction. They saw me pump my fists in the air and tears well in my eyes. They filmed my parents hugging me and people giving me high fives. What they didn't capture was how I felt on the inside, and those feelings were like nothing I had experienced before. Sure, there were lots of little wins and fun moments along the way, but in that moment everything I had gained flashed before my eyes. I had found and stayed true to my values. I had met an outlandish goal without having any idea how I was going to do it when I began. I never veered from my course. I refused to let challenges, adults, or my own limited thinking get in my way. I had beaten some politicians at their own game and teamed up with others. I had rallied the media, used storytelling, and repeated catchy soundbites to inspire action. I felt empowered and deeply satisfied.

And then Vern Fernsby asked for order and called out my name.

Everyone quieted.

"You know, the first time you called my house, I thought you were just some kid who'd go away. You never went away, and I have to tell you, I am proud of what you have done for Brutus and Ursula. I think we all are."

I would never have expected to hear those words out of Vern's mouth. It was as if he held up a white flag, declaring a truce after our long battle. I saw his humanity for the first time. I realized that the man who I had always seen as my archnemesis and the villain in the bears' story was neither of those things. He had his own agenda and I had mine. Luckily for the bears and for the sake of our conscience, my agenda prevailed. The front page of the *Sacramento Bee* said it all the next morning. The headline read: "Teen Triumphs in Battle for Bears."

It would take five months before Brutus and Ursula would actually be moved, a time that spanned the end of my sophomore year, that summer of '98 and the beginning of my junior year. I stayed committed to my activism, but without money to raise or a single project to focus on, my work became lots of street protests and dressing up. I wore a horse costume and stood in front of the drugstore to protest the selling of pregnant horse urine to menopausal women. I spent a weekend in front of the Republican National Convention dressed as a pig and insisted they tax meat. I dropped banners over the freeway on Thanksgiving. I protested fur outside of Macy's on Black Friday and stuffed the racks of fur coats with photos of animal carcasses at Nordstrom as my mom shopped for shoes.

My friends at school didn't really get what I was doing. They had been into the bear project because it was cool to see me on TV, but none of them felt the passion that I did for animal rights. It bothered me that I had been unable to convince them to stop eating meat, so one Friday I invited them all over for movie night. Little did they know the VHS was from PETA and the movie was undercover footage from a particularly terrible slaughterhouse. It worked! They went vegetarian!

I was delighted that one video was all it took—until one day at lunch when Erinn ordered a chicken patty, her old mainstay. At first, I was disappointed, but I thought about all the futile fights I had with my dad at the dinner table and the discussions I had had with Sybil about accepting people with different beliefs and I decided to chill out. I had learned something over the years: you can't force anyone into anything, and the best way to change minds is to share your knowledge, lead by example, and have patience. Erinn knew how cruel meat was but she decided that she was okay with that. I loved her anyway. I was just happy that she tried vegetarianism for as long as she did. One month was better than none.

The day finally arrived for Brutus and Ursula to move. The bears' home at Folsom Zoo was complete and ready for them. My mom drove me to their old cage by the creek early that morning. I was surrounded by a large mob of media and cameras that watched my every move. Brutus and Ursula, anxious from all the commotion, paced around their cage. I wasn't sure who was more nervous about it all, me or the bears. I couldn't believe that the day had finally arrived, and I was worried the bears wouldn't make it.

I watched as a team of vets shot tranquilizer darts into Brutus's and Ursula's butts, and soon Brutus fell to the ground, his face smacking the cement. I wept with concern. The vets entered the cage to check the bears' vital signs, poke them for blood, and prepare them for the big move. At one point, one of the vets waved me into their cage. I crawled through the small door and crouched down next to Brutus. I touched his coarse fur for the first time and felt his rib cage rise and fall. He was such a large and majestic animal. I looked around and couldn't believe how small their cage felt from the inside. I couldn't wait to get out of there and I wondered where Brutus and Ursula had found the will to survive in that horrible place for so long.

It took seven of us to lift Brutus and then Ursula onto gurneys. Brutus would travel in a cage in the back of a Fish and Game pickup truck and Ursula would be in a hitched trailer. My mom and I trailed the truck, and I cried with joy the whole way to Folsom Zoo. I was so happy for the bears. They would never face another flood or have to slip on a slime-coated floor. They could enjoy bear things for the first time. They could roll around in their sandy dens and experience trees and grass. They would feast on fresh fruit and the occasional roadkill. I was happy for them and for what they represented. They were an important reminder that all animals, like all humans, deserve kindness and to be free. Brutus and Ursula also gave people a chance to speak up and discover they could be a force for good, even with just a twenty-five-cent donation. I hoped everyone who had heard their story learned how important it was to shed light on any kind of abuse, and that it was possible to make things better for the ones we walk with. Not by waiting, not by shaking our heads, but by having a vision, busting through challenges and being unconcerned about how long it might take.

The bears thrived in their new home at Folsom Zoo. Brutus would dive into his pool after fish and forage for kibble in the tall grasses, while Ursula would lie in the dirt and sunbathe for hours. The media kept calling my house for months after their relocation. *Teen People* named me "One of Twenty Teens Who Will Change the World"; Animal Planet sent a crew to tell the story of the bear's *Wild Rescue*; and then I got the call of my dreams—from Nickelodeon. They had a brand-new game show called *Figure It Out* and they wanted to fly me to Florida to meet Olympic gold medalist Summer Sanders and a panel of Nickelodeon stars who'd have to guess what I had done for the bears. There were cash prizes and international trips up for grabs. I imagined I would finally meet Clarissa and see how slime was made. I couldn't believe that I was actually going to be on the TV network I had watched so religiously as a kid. My dad agreed to go with me on the trip and there was a production date set. One of the Nickelodeon producers called me to explain how everything would work.

"When you finally reveal what you have done for the bears, we are going to have two bears and their trainer join you on the set," he said.

I literally gasped. "Oh, absolutely not."

The work I did for the bears was not an isolated campaign. It was about teaching people reverence for all living things. I would never eat meat again, I'd always buy cruelty-free products, and I would definitely not appear on TV with two bears who were most likely whipped and shackled when the cameras weren't rolling. I explained to them that I believed in the rights of all animals and I told them I would not be coming to Florida.

I was deeply disappointed in Nickelodeon but realized I had outgrown all their programming anyway. Now I had a friend like Clarissa—a whole group of them, in fact. We'd go downtown, show up to parties. They made life in the suburbs tolerable.

We all went to *Spice World* on opening night, and that film changed my life in ways nearly as profound as my work with the bears had. I sang at the top of my lungs during the film, and afterward I begged my parents to let me go to London. I wanted to hunt down and photograph all the film's locations—Royal Albert Hall, Big Ben, Tower Bridge—and get a taste of Britain.

At school, I was catching my fair share of attention. The same month the superintendent of the school district honored me for my work with the bears, I was called into the vice principal's office.

"Why am I getting calls from the SPCA?" Mr. Sophia asked me, shutting the door to his office.

"I asked Ms. Clark where the cats they are dissecting in biology come from and she said the SPCA. I called the SPCA and asked if that was true. It wasn't, so you might want to pull Ms. Clark into your office, not me," I said.

There was nothing he could say about my call to the SPCA, and nothing he could do when one day during lunch I danced on top of one of the lunch tables while the Spice Girls blared over the speakers. He just stood there screaming at me to get down. Once the song was over, I stepped down but kept dancing in his face. I felt proud and powerful and I knew the vice principal, like many of the other adults with whom I had faced off, couldn't touch me. I had learned that they thought they were more powerful than us kids, but they really weren't. He ushered me, in my tight shiny pants and disco shirt, to the doorway of the front office. He was blushing and mad.

"I don't want to see you dancing on a table ever again," he insisted.

His raised voice didn't scare me a bit, but I agreed—and knew with even more certainty that I had to get out of Elk Grove.

My parents ended up letting me go to London that summer for a month. They paid for me to stay with some family from an exchange program who lived two hours outside of the city. The mom could care less about what I did and would let me take the two-hour train into London every day. The excitement I felt every time that train pulled into Paddington Station never faded over those four weeks. Every day brought an adventure. I explored new neighborhoods, ate at all the cool vegetarian restaurants, and got a kick out of the local slang. I loved how vibrant and diverse London was. The Underground—or "the tube," as they called it—brought everyone together. The tube gave me access to the entire city and let me see how spirited a place could be.

I usually caught the Circle Line to the Piccadilly Line directly to the West End, the entertainment district. I watched *Grease*, *Chicago*, and *Les Misérables* onstage and experienced the theatrics of my first gay pride parade. I was surrounded by rainbows and people dancing in the streets. I snuck into bars on Old Compton Street. I took a slow boat down the Thames to set my watch to Greenwich mean time. I woke my mom up with the news from a pay phone.

"Mom. You've got to set all the clocks in the house," I told her, completely ignoring the fact that it was 4:12 a.m. in California. "It's twelve minutes past the hour right... *now.*" She set all the clocks in our house and with a slightly groggy voice asked me how my day was.

"I saw the latest Spice Girl music video today at Tower Records," I told her, and insisted she find the track and listen to it. She ran downstairs and played it on my CD player. *Mama* was a sweet song about moms just wanting the best for their kids and it couldn't have been more perfectly timed. I was so far from her, I missed her, and those lyrics said it all. "She used to be my only enemy and never let me be free / Catching me in places that I knew I shouldn't be / Every other day I crossed the line I didn't mean to be so bad / I never thought you would become the friend I never had." I was touched by those lyrics and realized that despite all our fights and her long restrictions, she had always done her best by me and that all she did was love me. I stood there at that pay phone, surrounded by tourists setting their watches to Greenwich time, singing the lyrics I could faintly hear over the phone as my mom listened along and cried.

"Mama, I love you," I sang to her.

"I love you too, honey," she sniffled.

My obsession with the Spice Girls and my trip to London may have seemed superficial, but it wasn't. Being free and so far from the suburbs was as important to me as my time in Costa Rica, only better because London felt like the middle of the universe. I went to Paris by train, and Wales to meet my distant family. I saw that the world was big and colorful and generous. I wanted to see it all, dance in the streets, and most importantly on that trip, find a pair of six-inch platforms. Ginger Spice always killed that look, and she was my favorite. I ended up buying size thirteen Buffalo boots with money my dad wired me for a pair. He knew those shoes were more than a fashion statement for me. They made me six feet, seven inches tall. I loved seeing the world from that height, rocking around the streets of London, full of optimism and pride.

When I came home, I told my parents I wanted to go to university in London. I wanted that freedom and that world to be mine. I thought about Brutus and Ursula a lot while I was there. As soon as my jet lag had worn off—which took a few days—I spent an afternoon with them. I sat on the bench across from their enclosure watching Ursula. Her head rested on her two paws. She slept peacefully in her den, trying to beat that late summer heat. I was grateful for her and Brutus. They inspired me to see the world and myself in a different way. They helped me to discover strengths I never knew I had. They allowed me to speak my truth and spread a message of compassion. I sat there and wished that Ursula and Brutus could understand all that they had done for me.

"Thank you," I whispered.

Epilogue

A few months after my visit with Ursula, she was found in her den with her hindquarters partially paralyzed. We learned she had a degenerative disease of the spine. A lifetime of living on concrete, a bad diet, and the inability to move had taken its toll on her body. Luckily, her keepers at Folsom Zoo loved her and did everything they could to help her live a good life. She was the most trusting bear, allowing acupuncturists to poke her and masseurs to touch her. She had weekly sessions of Reiki and worked with a physical therapist who would coax her into her warm pool to stretch, tone, and strengthen her muscles. Her living conditions had improved, but four years after she moved to Folsom she came down with an incurable skin infection. Her quality of life was so diminished that the zoo decided to let her go peacefully.

Lea had left the Sacramento Zoo and was Ursula's primary keeper at Folsom. In Ursula's obituary, she said the sibling bears had "truly been gifts" to their caretakers and that Ursula proved that intimate human-animal partnerships that might at first seem implausible are possible. "She brought us joy and friendship and was told daily how precious she was," Lea said.

Just a year later, another obituary landed in the *Sacramento Bee*:

> Brutus, the black bear whose public face earned him many human friends, was euthanized by his veterinarian at the Folsom City Zoo Sanctuary late Wednesday.

I was grief-stricken. I was sad to know I would never see Brutus or Ursula again, but I was happy they had a chance to retire, eat delicious food, and experience the goodness of humans for a while. I hoped they were together again in some place where there were no cages.

I loved what I learned and who I met on my journey with those bears. My sadness about their deaths faded and their obituaries became important relics for me. Their eulogies were longer than those for most humans and represented why I started my work in the first place: to give animals a voice, to help them to be seen, to allow their pain to be ours, and to make us pause if only for a moment, to mourn their passing.

Luckily their deaths did not mean the end of the black bear enclosure at the Folsom Zoo. Three orphaned bears now call Folsom Zoo home and a sweet young bear named Henry lives where Brutus and Ursula once did. He followed his mother into a public campsite and Fish and Game decided that they would both have to be euthanized. There was a public outcry to save Henry and luckily there was space for him at Folsom Zoo. Despite his traumatic beginnings, he has blossomed into a wonderful, charismatic and happy bear. Thanks to my mom raising a fuss, a plaque about Brutus and Ursula is permanently affixed to the fence in front of his cage so visitors who never got a chance to meet them can still at least know their story.

I ended up moving to London for university and convinced myself that I would become a TV reporter. I imagined I would uncover the world's injustices, one news report at a time. I applied and got an internship at the London bureau of CBS News while I studied. My start date was September 12, 2001. I watched as the US war in Afghanistan raged across the monitors that filled an entire wall of the newsroom. The raw footage that streamed into that bureau and what the public saw on CBS News were two very different things. I witnessed blood running in the streets, mass killings in sports stadiums, and the most gruesome side of humanity. I was overwhelmed by the horrors of war, how poorly the news covered it, and I decided TV wasn't for me.

I ended up moving to Sydney, Australia, where I finished my degree and filmed the many protests that happened throughout my college years. I witnessed activists ripping down fences that held back refugees, filmed lockdowns at US military bases, and documented people filling the streets in protest of a new war in Iraq. I lived in an amazing vegan commune with a bunch of activists. We debated what nonviolent direct action meant, closed down bridges with our bikes, and reclaimed the streets with music and dancing.

The dream of the '90s faded away and I learned that time wasn't the only thing that changed. I moved back to California and I ended up in San Francisco, where I lived in another communal house at the corner of Haight and

Ashbury. The 1960s counterculture movement began on those very streets, and it lived on. Rent was still cheap, and you couldn't walk down the street without meeting all sorts of interesting characters. I honed my storytelling powers and worked on ways to use film and media to educate people and inspire action. It only took me two years there to realize that I wasn't gay.

"I'm queer," I told everyone.

Queer feels like a better identity for me because I learned something important about myself: that I could love all sorts of people and gender was just one aspect of being human. I met an amazing woman, who I married. We found love, and that's what really matters. We have a sweet dog named Beatrice who reminds me of a little black bear. We named our son Noah and we joke that if we have a girl one day, we will name her Ursula.

Not too long ago, I met Nancy Knight for coffee— she was the woman from the Sacramento Zoo who had threatened me with a lawsuit. She had spent her life keeping animals behind bars, so she was right up there with Cruella de Vil in my eyes. I met her mostly out of curiosity for what my adult self would think of her all those years later. As we talked over our soy lattes, I was shocked when she told me how pleased she was by the news that

Ringling Brothers Circus had ended their elephant acts and that SeaWorld was struggling in the wake of *Blackfish*, the damning film about how abusive captivity is for whales. It made me realize that Nancy was an animal person like me and that we were not so different after all.

It also made me think of all those warm evenings I spent protesting outside of Ringling Brothers Circus when it came to Sacramento. At the time, I wondered if our chants and colorful signs mattered and if protesting in the streets could actually evoke change. I showed up every August, just in case, and after three long decades of sustained protests by caring citizens, I had my answer: Ringling Brothers Circus didn't just end their animal acts, they closed the circus forever. No elephants will be dragged around the country anymore and the fiery hoops the big cats were forced to jump through are now extinguished forever.

I still dance around to the Spice Girls and have stayed in touch with Jane Goodall. She is the only person over the years who is still curious about Bear Boy. We don't talk much, but she always makes an effort to send a letter or an email saying hello. One day, I learned that she sends five hundred letters a year to kids like me—people she's met who carry on her spirit. When I heard that, it confirmed her status as my hero. Not because she appears on the cover of magazines, or because she publishes books, or because her films win awards. It's because she has brought the jungle to us and has allowed us to see that everything is connected. She advocates for human prisoners and zoo animals. She has dedicated every waking hour to spreading her message of peace, equality, environmentalism, and animal rights. Most important, though, is her faith in young people and her belief in their power to create a better world.

Jane is a true grassroots activist, and we need more people like her. There seems to be so much wrong in our world these days and things can feel pretty overwhelming, but the world needs strong voices to speak up for those who can't—and people like you to stand up for what you believe in.

What is important to *you*?

Who will *you* stand up for?

How will *you* make the world a better place?

ACKNOWLEDGMENTS

Jennie Nash, you are a fabulous human, book coach, and editor. This book would have never existed without you. I am so grateful for you and all your support in my story and writing process. You have been such a champion, a cheerleader, and a shining light. You've helped me feel so damn empowered and see that deadlines and 4 a.m. writing sessions pay off.

Bridget Sumser—I love you. You are an amazing wife. Thank you for being patient with this journey. I could not have told this story without your companionship and support. Thank you for accepting me, loving me, and helping me better understand myself. We are co-creating a beautiful life and family. For that, I am forever indebted.

Noah—you are such a bright and enthusiastic light. To many hikes, belly laughs, dances under the disco ball, and stories yet told.

Doaly, you are a fantastic collaborator, artist, and storyteller. Being part of your creative process was a real dream. I love the art you created for this book.

Carla Weise, you created a perfect layout and you rolled with the punches. Thank you.

Ray Sumser, Jamie Jensen, Joyce Maynard, and Dorsey Griffith, thanks for encouraging me and helping me write thoughtful and compelling jacket copy.

Amy Van der Molen, Carrie Ziser, Anna Ziser, Eli Ziser, and Kate Sumser, thanks for being the first to read this book, sharing your thoughts, and cheering me on.

I am sending lots of love to my family and friends, who have always been exceptional. Erinn Floyd, thanks for being the BFF I never had. Rachel Gregg, I am so grateful for you and your always thoughtful perspective. Roy Belcher, thanks for making me laugh. I love we share Facetime with the boys, questionable taste in music, and that we get to experience papahood together.

Dad, thank you for taking me to the mall and letting me buy all the polyester and platforms I could imagine. That's what I call acceptance. Berta, thanks for always supporting this journey and staying curious about the process. Mom, thanks for teaching me about the positive impact we each have the power to make. Colleen, thank you for being a great nana and pod-mate. This book would have never been possible without your love and the thousands of hours you have spent with Noah.

To Robin, Cody, and the rest of the crew—This book took ten years to write, but your inspiring words and endless inspiration helped me through 2020—I laughed and cried to the finish line.

To you, the reader. Thanks for getting this far and reading this book to the very end. I'd love to hear from you.

ROBIN WEIR

JUSTIN BARKER wants you to stand up for yourself and your fellow earthlings. He loves the Spice Girls, and he thinks zoos are the worst. He is a San Francisco-based TV producer, writer, and activist. Justin and his wife, Bridget, are parents to Noah and their rescued pup, Beatrice, and are queer AF. They believe #LoveisLove, #BlackLivesMatter, and thirst for a more just and equitable world.

justinbarker.tv

Twitter: @justinbarkertv

Instagram: @justinbarkertv

CPSIA information can be obtained
at www.ICGtesting.com
Printed in the USA
LVHW040618190522
719127LV00009B/1266

9 781736 084328